THE JOY
OF KINDNESS

THE JOY OF KINDNESS

Robert J. Furey

CROSSROAD · NEW YORK

1993
The Crossroad Publishing Company
370 Lexington Avenue, New York, NY 10017

Library of Congress Cataloging-in-Publication Data

Furey, Robert J.
    The joy of kindness / Robert J. Furey.
        p.   cm.
    Includes bibliographical references.
    ISBN 0-8245-1269-3 (pbk.)
    1. Kindness.   I. Title.
BJ1533.K5F87   1993
177'.7—dc20   92-38935
                                                        CIP

To my brothers and sisters:
Diane, Richard, Bill, Maureen,
Susan, and Karen.
And to my daughter Kelly.

CONTENTS

Preface   ix

1 · THE KINDNESS VINE   1

2 · THE ROOTS OF KINDNESS   18

3 · GETTING WARM   37

4 · HEROES AND VILLAINS   56

5 · FORGIVENESS   78

6 · HEALING   98

7 · TRANSFORMATIONS   121

8 · GRATITUDE   142

Notes   153

PREFACE

The Joy of Kindness was, in its earliest stages, a book designed to answer the question: why are kind people kind? At the time I felt, and still do, that this is as important a question as one could attempt to answer. As the material started to come together, however, a second, related and equally important, purpose emerged. Could the written word help people develop compassion? Then, finally, the two paths merged as I realized that if one comes to understand kindness, one will feel the need to share it. In the case of kindness, understanding and sharing are inseparable.

Those who make compassion an essential part of their lives find the joy of life. Kindness deepens the spirit and produces rewards that cannot be completely explained in words. It is an experience more powerful than words. To become acquainted with kindness one must be prepared to learn new things and feel new feelings. Kindness is more than a philosophy of the mind. It is also a philosophy of the spirit.

In a recent survey, people of all ages were asked what they had learned in their lives. A sixty-six-year-old replied: "I've learned that the best advice you can give anyone is, 'Be Kind.'"[1] What follows supports this simple wisdom.

To get the most out of reading what lies ahead, I suggest you find a bookmark that gives you some room to write. Before you begin chapter 1, jot down the names of people in your life who you believe personify generosity and caring. Then add words or symbols that remind you of specific encounters you've had with kindness, even if you witnessed them only from a distance. As you read this book, I encourage you to continue to add names and memories. Use as many bookmarks as you need.

I hope you will benefit from what you read. I know you will benefit from what you write.

1

THE KINDNESS VINE

No act of kindness, however small, is ever wasted.
Aesop

I can't say for sure when kindness began. I know it arrived on the planet long before any of us did and I hope it will remain well after we're gone. But I guess that will be largely up to us. It seems that somewhere in time one generation began handing it down to the next and that's pretty much the process we've followed ever since.

Unfortunately, some generations have handed down less than they were given. These were the eras that found other things to appreciate. They protected what they had and learned to hoard, fence in, keep an eye on, assert, defend, and isolate. They built noble-sounding philosophies to support their ways and even tried to create societies that could survive without generosity. After all, they reasoned, if all the poor people starve, there will be no more poverty. And if all those who cannot take care of themselves are permitted to wither away, we may wipe out illness altogether.

Then there have been generations that have revered another set of values. They maintained an awareness of the needs of others and supported and respected each other's sacrifices. They built their communities on cooperation and saw to it that their children were surrounded with examples of altruism. They seemed to understand that we're all in this together.

1

These cultures of compassion have represented the highest peaks in the history of human civilization.

While we can point to the past and debate which eras fell into which categories, the confusion really begins when we start to examine our present condition. How close are we to becoming a culture of compassion? Many say that we need to become a "kinder, gentler nation." Kinder and gentler than what? The way we were before? Kinder and gentler than other nations? Or maybe it means that we should be constantly evolving in the direction of being kinder and gentler. If so, I wonder if the present generation will move us forward.

This is a book about people and kindness. Kindness, of course, has many characteristics and a variety of names such as love, generosity, altruism, care, and compassion. If you are a kind person, this is a book *about* you. If you are trying to become a kind—or kinder—person, this is a book *for* you. And if you are someone who does not believe in compassion or sees no need for generosity, well . . . it probably doesn't matter because if this is the case, you haven't read this far anyway.

What I hope to accomplish before we are through is to realize the meaning of kindness. This is not to say, however, that kindness will ever be explained. I don't know if that's possible. It's more than words. To grasp the meaning of kindness you must develop all your senses. You might even have to develop new senses. Antoine de Saint Exupéry may have said it best toward the end of The Little Prince: "And now here is my secret, a very simple secret: It is only with the heart that one can see rightly; what is essential is invisible to the eye."

Kindness may be the simplest truth of all. Still, it cannot be completely described. I suspect that an inevitable criticism of this book will be that it leaves certain significant points unexplained. But some of the most important lessons in life can only be understood as long as they are not explained. Kindness, it seems, is meant to be acted upon rather than merely discussed.

Don't wait for words to capture the meaning and power of kindness; they never will.

The Vine

A vine grows in this part of the universe, a vine like no other. Its health has always been less than stable, sometimes flourishing and at other times withering. It belongs to no particular season, climate, or terrain. It can survive the most destructive environments or see its growth stopped in conditions that seem ideal.

This vine is the vine of human kindness—the Kindness Vine. The Kindness Vine has been with us a long, long time. It has survived wars, famine, and every type of tragedy imaginable. During the Holocaust in Europe during World War II when millions of innocents were being slaughtered, thousands of brave souls risked their lives, as well as the lives of their families, to rescue strangers. Through history's darkest hours, while its branches were cut and burned and gassed, the Vine lived on.

Equally remarkable, however, is the fact that the Vine has not sent its branches farther and deeper. It seems to be giving us the opportunity to nurture and raise it; yet, as a people, we sometimes appear afraid that it may get out of control. Somewhere inside us we feel an urge so strong to live compassionately that we can fear the thought of this force being released. So most of us keep it in check and, if we release it at all, it tends to be in calculated doses.

When Albert Camus wrote, "To state quite simply what we learn in time of pestilence . . . there are more things to admire in men than to despise," he accurately estimated the human situation. So too did Mother Teresa when she said, "The greatest disease of mankind is the absence of love." Little value comes from debating whether human beings are basically good or evil. Our daily experience provides ample support for both views. What deserves our attention is the fact that humans have the capacity for great compassion. Furthermore we have a powerful need to be compassionate, and until this need is met, we can never truly find contentment.

With each act of kindness the Vine grows stronger. Most of its growth comes in inches. Although not apparent to the five primary senses, it can be felt by those who allow themselves to feel. Being wrapped in its branches produces a feeling of joy and serenity that cannot be imagined by those who have not experienced it. And there is no greater despair than that which comes to those who have never touched the Vine.

The future of humanity depends on the health of the Kindness Vine. In spite of its awesome resiliency, we cannot rely on this force being able to sustain itself alone. Like all forms of life, its survival depends, at least in part, on its environment. The root of the Kindness Vine has demonstrated a tremendous will and ability to survive. Its branches, however, can be fragile, retreating with the slightest insult. It seems that each generation inherits a turn to care for the Vine.

Caring for the Vine requires, more than anything, a *desire* to do so. It calls for a deliberate commitment to help it grow. The quality of life on our planet depends on the health of the Kindness Vine. As the Vine grows, so too do we. As a result, we have our own health and happiness in our hands. Should we use our hands and our hearts to tend to this miraculous plant, the Vine of human compassion will connect us with all of humanity.

Kindness

Kindness, love, altruism, caring, generosity, and compassion all describe acts of giving. These are not motivated by the promise of reward. For now, we need only understand that they find energy in the conviction that caring for the world and the people in it represents the right way to live.

Psychologists Jacqueline R. Macaulay and Leonard Berkowitz have offered the following as a definition of altruism or, as they call it, "prosocial behavior": "Behavior carried out to benefit another without anticipation of rewards from external sources." More recently, behavioral scientist Morton Hunt expanded the Macaulay-Berkowitz definition and described altruism as "behavior carried out to benefit another at some sacrifice to oneself, and without, or not primarily because of, the expectation of rewards from external sources."[1]

We can begin with these theories. Kindness, at its most basic level, means acting charitably without requiring or expecting to be rewarded for one's deed. Later we will move a little deeper and consider other aspects of kindness such as the need to care for yourself. We will explore the idea that kindness may never be understood by relying on biological or psychological formulas. We will also address why many, perhaps most, social scientists refuse to believe in the existence of genuine altruism. Ultimately, we will deal with compassion's spiritual dimension.

It might appear that we could cut through all the questions and arguments surrounding kindness by going straight to the source. If we could just round up the kindest people we could find and interrogate them on the cause and nature of their behavior, we might find all the answers. But as if to prove that life insists on preserving a certain amount of mystery, these generous persons are usually unable to identify their source (or sources). In other words, I have found what others before me have concluded—kind folks have few words when it comes to explaining their ways. Morton Hunt succinctly summarized his findings in this area by remarking, "Altruists themselves know very little about why they behave as they do."[2] Similarly, after studying a group of especially generous millionaires, sociologist Paul Schervish reported that he had run into a "dead end." He could not find a "clean motive" for their generosity. Instead, he received only brief explanations such as, "I want to give something back."[3]

In fact, if you ask generous people about their generosity, they tend to become embarrassed, almost as if no one was supposed to have noticed. If they can articulate any response at all it usually amounts to something like, "It just seems like the right thing to do." Occasionally, they will identify a person in their lives who served as a role model and who planted the seeds of kindness in them. This person may have been a parent or a grandparent who appeared to find contentment through caring. This might suggest that children learn compassion not so much from being told but rather by being touched.

This reluctance to dwell on their noble acts teaches us at least two important facts about kindness. First, it contains within it much humility. Caring souls find little use in calling attention to themselves. They are less involved with their own egos. They connect and empathize so well with others that they are unlikely to consider themselves more newsworthy than anyone else. In short, if you ask truly humble people what makes them so special, you probably won't get much of an answer. This humility, however, should never be confused with a lack of insight. Actually, one could argue that kindness reflects a profound insight into life.

Second, people with strong altruistic tendencies prefer to act out their convictions. They would rather "walk the walk" than merely "talk the talk." They remind us that compassion does not need justification. To giving people, the question "Why do you care?" may be like asking "Why do fish swim?" or "Why do birds fly?" They do so because that is what they are here to do.

Thus we have gathered two important clues into the nature of kindness: it includes humility and it involves action. Interestingly, the humility can camouflage the deed. Consequently, we can underestimate the goodness of people. For example, you might be surprised to know:

—Every year about nine million Americans give one or more pints of blood to benefit people they've never met.

—Nearly half of all American adults do some kind of volunteer work.

—People in seven out of ten American households contribute to charities.[4]

I guess only a few of those nine million folks wear their "I Gave Blood" buttons. For the most part, they just roll down their sleeves and go about their business. Giving blood is such a quiet procedure that we rarely hear all those donations being made. It is another example of the silence of kindness. It grows as quietly as a Vine.

Human Nature

In a recent study, 83 percent of blood donors indicated a willingness to undergo anesthesia and stay overnight in a hospital in order to donate bone marrow to a stranger.[5] And even though blood donors may indeed be a select group of especially generous people, as we have already seen, this group of charitable individuals numbers in the millions. At the very least, if we were to accurately judge the goodness of humanity, we would conclude that we have a solid foundation of compassionate souls. A foundation with the power to build upon itself. You see, kindness is contagious. Unfortunately, so are cruelty and indifference.

One of the most consistent findings in the study of human behavior is that we tend to imitate what we see. Thus, compassion begets compassion while inconsideration tends to produce more of the same. After hearing news stories of violence and cruelty, we are less likely to go out of our way to help someone else. But if we see someone drop money in the FEED THE HOMELESS canister, we are more likely to do the same. Study after study has documented this phenomenon. Kindness, like cruelty and indifference, is contagious. The more we encounter it, the kinder we become.

One possible explanation for this state of affairs concerns your view of yourself. If you're not sure whether you're supposed to be a giver or a taker, you tend to follow those who seem to know. Until you make up your own mind, you will need to be led. Once you decide, however, you will be the one who leads.

For centuries scholars have asked the question, "Are we, as human beings, basically generous and caring or are we, in the final analysis, selfish?" If you tried to research this issue, you could go to the libraries and study what the great minds have written. You would not, however, find much controversy among the tribe that calls itself scientists. For the most part, the biological and social sciences have denied the existence of genuine kindness. Instead they suggest, indeed insist, that an individual will behave altruistically *only* if rewarded for doing so. This reward may come in the form of recognition and praise or the expectation that one has fulfilled an obligation and now has the right to expect similar treatment. Somehow, somewhere (so the theory goes), there must be a payoff.

And although this may be the majority view, it is not the only perspective. Earlier in the twentieth century, Alfred Adler and then Carl Rogers voiced the opinion that humans are quite capable of self-sacrifice for no other reason than the welfare of our fellow beings. Contemporary scholars such as Leo Buscaglia, Bernie S. Siegel, Morton Hunt, and Alfie Kohn have all asserted that we are quite capable of genuine empathy and concern for others and that, beyond this, not only can we sacrifice for the sake of others, but only by doing so can we fulfill our potential and become what we are meant to be.

As the debate continues among the sages, we must deal with this issue in our own way. In spite of the attention this question has received, I don't think it's that important. No one can honestly tell you if you are "basically" good or evil. You decide. You can be either. From infancy on we demonstrate the capacity for complete selfishness *and* unlimited compassion. Although kindness may be the more correct and meaningful road, it is not the only road. Although we were born with a heart, we can choose to be heartless.

The question of whether we are fundamentally good or evil can make for interesting classroom-like conversation. But it's not really that important. Much more crucial is the personal choice concerning how you will conduct your life. The more significant query aims itself at each of us. *Are you choosing to be a giver or a taker?* This is not a question to be bandied about in an eggheaded way (i.e., if we don't answer it today, we'll get back to it later). It's too important to leave unanswered. And this is the key. *It's not our place to dwell on the question. Rather, it's our responsibility to answer it.* Life itself asks if we are choosing to be givers or takers. It makes little sense for us to keep repeating the question. We each have to answer it for ourselves.

Your decision will impact many. Caring, remember, is contagious. This puts a little more pressure on the first person to act. What I mean is that if the first person in line at the grocery store, for example, puts a donation in the Diabetes Foundation can, there is a greater chance that those behind her will also. But if she doesn't, well . . .

We are all the first in line at one time or in one way or another. And what we do influences everyone else. Small acts like walking your neighbor's mail over to their house or dropping a quarter in as someone's parking meter runs out have an effect. Every act of kindness improves the world.

We are all born into a world that needs us. We find ourselves in harmony with our world when we try to fill these needs. I once read that patients in nursing homes tend to have improved health if they are given a plant to care for. Our world needs us and we seem to need to care for something.

It appears that human nature *fits* with the ways of the universe.

What Have You Seen?

If you told me how much kindness you've known in your life, I just might be able to tell you how happy you are. Not that caring for people can protect you from sorrow. Even the most fortunate people have crosses to bear. As crazy as it may sound, real happiness does not mean an absence of sorrow. Real contentment acknowledges the existence of tragedy. It refuses to conclude, however, that there is *only* sorrow. Those of us who have been most frequently reminded of the love and caring the world can offer are those most likely to hold on to true serenity.

Some of us have had much kindness brought right to us. In a healthier world, this would be the birthright of all children. But this is too often not the case. Certain events, however, are so necessary to healthy human development that even when they are not provided they must be pursued and discovered. Love and caring and kindness are such events. These qualities put the humanness in humanity.

Everyone benefits from an encounter with caring. To those who are familiar with kindness each new encounter serves as a reminder and, hopefully, strengthens the conviction that life is worth living to the fullest. These folks become healthier and happier each time they touch kindness. But to the souls who have never received the care they need, an encounter with honest compassion can bring on substantial change. One's world becomes altered once kindness introduces itself.

In either case, one simple principle applies. Before we will accept the reality of sincere human compassion, we must open ourselves to at least the possibility that it exists. You may not need to absolutely believe in order to see it, but you may need to open yourself to the *possibility* that it exists. Once someone becomes convinced that "no one really cares" or that "everyone is out only for themselves," then (until that person's mind is changed) kindness may not live in his or her world.

People who live in cruel or uncaring environments live in fear. Because of the fear, they are reluctant to put themselves through the vulnerability that comes with change. Instead they remain rigid and isolated, protecting themselves from all the things that might hurt.

If we are to grow into the happiest, healthiest people we can be—people capable of bringing health and happiness to others as well—then we must be able to absorb kindness. This can be as unsettling as it is marvelous. Nonetheless, we will grow only if we allow ourselves to be moved. Experiencing the power of kindness changes us. It moves us to a better place.

In trying to find the meaning of kindness, I have spoken to a wide variety of people from many walks of life. Some time ago I asked a group of elementary and high school teachers, who were attending a workshop I gave, to share their ideas. Their thoughts ranged from the sublime to the ridiculous.

A fourth-grade teacher who appeared to be in her mid-twenties immediately recalled advice given to her as a child: "My mother always said, 'If someone is being mean and nasty to you, kill them with kindness!'" Having said this with a huge smile on her face, she sat down. No explanation added. Like many statements about kindness, this one seemed to end with the unspoken, "If you don't understand, you won't understand."

A middle-aged woman gave a more sober reply: "Kindness is accepting and liking myself. . . . It is an attitude that influences my entire perception. When I am able to experience kindness, I appreciate and enjoy my kinship with mankind." A younger male teacher remarked that "kind actions are remembered over a long period of time." Another participant reminded me that "kindness can mean anything from giving a hug to giving a kidney."

The wisest people around maintain a respect for simple wisdom. They know that the most profound insights don't always produce a "Wow!" Observations and gestures so subtle that they can be easily missed may be the most common vessels of truth. There is, after all, such a thing as profound simplicity.

Once, for example, a group of scientists found a blind pelican. Although the implications of this might be lost on most of us, the scientists were amazed. How, they wondered, could this unsighted bird survive? You see, pelicans eat fish. They must dive, head first, into the water to catch their meals. So how can a blind pelican endure?

The scientists learned that this pelican survived through the generosity of other pelicans. This benevolent community of birds fed their disabled brother. They wouldn't allow him to starve.[6] Now I realize this isn't the most powerful story ever told. In fact, it may seem quite insignificant. But as unimportant as this tale may sound, the image of this blind animal is quite a symbol. I guess symbols don't mean much, however, until one begins to appreciate the symbolism involved. Then they have a way of sticking with you.

The blind pelican can make one wonder about the impact of a needy soul. If a community moves to feed their blind pelicans, then maybe they all become better creatures. In other words, we may not be able to sustain a culture of kindness without a willingness to be both giver and grateful receiver. For instance, if this particular disabled bird had refused any assistance, he would have died. And so too might have his flock's willingness to help another brother or sister.

We will spend more time discussing gratitude later. Still, we need to begin to understand that gratitude helps foster compassion. The Vine may survive without gratitude but it will not reach its potential. This plant grows more readily in soil that respects and appreciates its presence.

Love and kindness are essential parts of our beings. Carl Jung believed that these qualities were part of our collective unconscious. Our collective unconscious, Jung claimed, contained the basics of human experience that lie rooted within each of us. These elements have existed from the beginning of time and have represented the essential ingredients in our personal and genetic survival and development. These traits include nurturing, loyalty, justice, generosity, forgiveness, and love.[7] Our expression of these qualities represents an expression of our true nature. With this honesty comes a courage and contentment that Shakespeare understood when he advised: "To thine own self be true."

Once this expression begins, it can feel as if it has a force of its own. You feel moved. Changes occur. Sometimes small changes. Sometimes large, sweeping changes that we might call transformations or awakenings. Those who realize their true selves, and who thus hear their callings, move toward the place that is right for them. Psychologists have described this state as self-actualization. Buddhists have named it satori. It has been detailed by many philosophies and religions. It is the place where things begin to come together in unity and one finds one's true direction and purpose in life.

You cannot buy a map to this place. Life will take you there. But only if you allow life to move you.

The Fear of Kindness

Of all the kind words I've ever heard spoken, the deepest, most moving and most sincere have come, I think, during eulogies. I guess it's safer. If you speak highly of someone after his death, there is not as much of a chance that he will disappoint you. Nor is it likely that he will cut you off and tell you that you are embarrassing him. And you don't have to worry about being hurt when the kindness is not returned.

Certainly there are reasons why we should save kind words for funerals. It's safer that way. It's easier to affirm the deceased. They don't stir feelings of jealousy within us. After a friend or acquaintance has died we no longer envy how fortunate they were. It's O.K. that they had more money or better looks or more successful children. It doesn't seem to matter anymore.

And though there may be some sense to this line of reasoning, it has an absurd ring about it. Somewhere the voice inside us says

"Don't wait." Like most advice given by that little voice inside us, it does not elaborate. Just "Don't wait." That's all. For those who don't trust the voice's wisdom, there exists evidence to support its message. We find this lesson in grief. Perhaps the greatest sorrow present in the wake of a loved one's death is the regret for all the things that *were never said*. Things that should have been. Things that needed saying. But were not. And survivors are left to consider the sad thought, "I wish I had."

Kindness at times requires courage. More than anything, it takes courage to get started. Apathy provides shelter. It's safe to say "I don't care." If we care, we feel compelled to act. And when we act we can be hurt. To be sure, few pains sting more than being rejected or ridiculed while attempting to help.

The person who doesn't want to contribute can choose from a plethora of reasons why not to get involved. For instance, one could rationalize away the desire to do good by convincing oneself that the little voice inside us is really talking to someone else.

We can convince ourselves that kindness is less than necessary. In fact, we do this quite often. We don't always like to believe that we need kindness. Needing others can be frightening because they can hurt us. Life would be much safer if we were each completely self-sufficient. But such is not the case. We cannot survive without kindness.

Caring can also be strangled by denial. If we deny the need, we will not act on it. We need to be caring beings. If we are not, we will never fit into our world. We also need to accept kindness. If we do not, we will never feel that we belong. And when all is said and done, kindness given and kindness received are somehow part of the same process. Like two halves of one pervasive spirit. A spirit capable of embracing everyone.

When we lose contact with this spirit, we develop a void inside ourselves. Then, even if we accomplish all our goals, we still cannot escape the emptiness. Mother Teresa called this condition "spiritual deprivation." An inner void cannot be stuffed with material objects. It can be filled only by an orientation toward giving.

People who feel lost tend to refind direction in their lives once they hear, and then respond to, the call to serve. Take, for example, the story of the young man who began to wonder if life had any meaning at all. Although told in many different ways, one version goes like this: On a cold winter day in the midst of confusion and despair, the young man walked through one of the poorest sections of his city. As he traipsed through the streets, he saw old people trying to sleep on the sidewalks and young children shivering in their inadequate clothing. He saw poverty, suffering, and hopelessness.

As he walked, his frustration grew until finally, in a cynical voice, he exclaimed: "God, how can you allow this to continue? Have you ever really cared? How can you sit back and do nothing while you watch all this?"

Then, for the first time in his life, he heard the voice of God. "I do care and I have done something. Something miraculous. I made *you*."

The story ends here with us left to speculate about how the young man responded to God's message. We hope he became empowered as he came to understand that he was part of the solution. But maybe he remained unchanged and merely scoffed, "Yea, right."

Just about everyone wants to see compassion. The problem is we often want to see it come from someone or someplace else. But, of course, the only way to insure that kindness lives on your planet is to put it there yourself. Remember, kindness is as contagious as selfishness. It takes only one person to start a wave. Once started, however, it can require many to stop the tide.

Who Is a Kind Person?

Earlier I suggested that kind people shy away from opportunities to describe their giving ways. To this point, we have identified two reasons that compassionate souls stay tight-lipped. First, they possess a humility that keeps them from making themselves the center of attention. They are less involved with their own egos. They would rather point to the tasks they believe important. Second, kind people tend to be action oriented. They would rather *do* than *talk*. They can become ill at ease when asked to detail their altruistic behavior.

But there exists a third reason many of the most caring people refuse to explain their good will. You see, good people don't always feel like good people. They are in touch with the other side of themselves that wants to be self-serving. They are so aware of this dimension that being singled out for their charity can make them feel guilty.

One of the most important points about kindness is that kind people have the same selfish desires as everyone else. What's remarkable is that they rise above these limitations. Still, they can feel like frauds when asked about their goodness. Inside they may feel like, "If you only knew!"

We can take this even a step further and argue that genuinely caring people feel their selfishness more than anyone else. People who are most in touch with the needs of the world may be the most likely to struggle to overcome feelings of selfishness.

When we realize the need for our gifts and services, we hear the call to provide what we can. When what is needed is more than what we can supply (a common occurrence), we feel frustrated, guilty, or inadequate. There are, however, methods to avoid seeing the needs. Nothing squelches altruism more than denial. But if we allow ourselves to see the need, we will feel the call to act. Those most in touch with the need hear the clearest call. Sometimes it feels as if we are being called to do more than we possibly can.

Besides humility and an orientation toward action, kind people often have lingering doubts about their goodness. Perhaps even more so than less generous folks. Even truly virtuous individuals have selfish impulses—probably just as strong as everyone else's. They are not without pettiness or envy. Like the rest of us, they live with the shadow side of human nature. The compassionate, however, distinguish themselves through the ability to rise above their selfishness. They transcend the urge that pushes us to look out only for "number one." Kindness always represents a victory.

If we tried to round up all those truly deserving of the term *kind*, we might not get many volunteers. People just don't seem to describe themselves this way. Kind is probably not something you call yourself. Rather, it seems to be something people call each other.

We each decide for ourselves who are the compassionate. We have this right. We can at any time give someone this noble compliment. Consideration must be given, however, to the fact that some people hide their generosity. Never forget the army of anonymous donors. They give in silence and, in the process, remind us that there is more caring than might be apparent.

We will become a kinder and gentler world through a willingness to give people the benefit of the doubt. Be willing to see kindness in others. Even if you are wrong, your mistake could help someone become a better person. As Goethe knew, "If we take man as he is, we make him worse; if we take him as he ought to be, we help him become it." Even when we cannot see kindness in a person, we can (if we look) always see its potential.

Finally, kindness is a process, not a product. It's not something the wizard can give you to have and hold for ever and ever. A way of traveling more than a destiny, kindness, if we live it, comes one day at a time. And every day, somewhere inside each of us, we decide how we will live.

I doubt anyone acts or feels kind all the time. It's hard to become great at kindness. Besides, it seems that once we set our sights on being great, we tend to end up being selfish. Maybe the best thing we can ever become is a good human being.

Not surprisingly, where you find good human beings, you will find the Kindness Vine.

2

THE ROOTS OF KINDNESS

The sole meaning of life is to serve humanity.
Leo Tolstoy

One of the first things we learn in life is how to think like a child. It's also one of the most important lessons we ever learn.

Problems that seem impossible to solve can simplify and become quite manageable when considered in a childlike state. Children have a knack for simplifying things into perspective. Their genius is their simplicity. Adults can have a difficult time with this. Children, for instance, can understand an Aesop fable. A grownup, on the other hand, will try to explain it. Adults think wisdom means sounding wise. Children don't think about their wisdom.

To children, and those older folks fortunate enough to have maintained the spirit and wisdom of youth, kindness is simply a way to live. It feels right. And that's enough. Children try to live kindness not because it is explained to them but, rather, because they have seen it and felt its warmth. Children learn compassion by being exposed to it. In an environment that provides ample love and caring, children learn kindness the same way fish learn to swim. It is a natural part of the growth process.

But never ask caring children why they are kind. Most likely, they will assume you don't understand. And they would be right. If you have to ask a child why, you obviously don't understand.

Fortunately, life teaches. Even before we develop a question, we can find important answers. Often life's lessons are taught by those too young to do too much explaining.

One such lesson comes from the oft-told story of the boy and the starfish. One day a man, walking along a beach, notices that a freak tide has washed ashore thousands of small starfish and left them to die. He also sees a small boy picking up the starfish one by one and tossing them back into the ocean.

When the man comes up to the boy, he asks, "There are so many starfish washed up here, what difference can the few you throw back make?" The boy then held up the starfish he had in his hand and replied, "It's sure going to make a lot of difference to this one!" The man was so impressed with the child's mission that he spent the rest of the afternoon helping the boy throw starfish back into the ocean.

There's a certain understanding that comes with being a child. A special sense that allows one to appreciate the value of small efforts. The fact that one cannot rescue every suffering creature does not diminish by one iota the attempts made to help a single, silent starfish. The lesson is simple: you do what you can. You keep doing what you can. Hopefully, more people will come along. If you're lucky, you may start a wave. Maybe even a wave large enough to return all those starfish to the sea. Maybe.

One of the most important (perhaps *the* most important) questions children need answered is, "Is the world a friendly place?" Children prepare themselves to live in the world as they see it. Although they observe only their little corner of the planet, they tend to conclude that what they see is what exists everywhere. Thus, a child who lives in the midst of cruelty and neglect is apt to believe that such are the inevitable circumstances of life. She will then do what she can to prepare herself to survive in this jungle.

If, however, she lives surrounded by a loving environment where people care for and support and encourage one another, she is more likely to develop a lifestyle that values compassion and generosity. This child will do more than protect herself and her own interests. She will apply her gifts and talents toward the well-being of humanity.

Children need to know that they live in a place that desperately needs their gifts. Clearly, they also need to learn how to protect themselves. It might be that the best we can do for our kids is help them learn to be caring people while living in a world that can sometimes be unkind. The lack of compassion that can be evidenced in the newspaper points to the need for contributions of caring. Generous souls belong everywhere. We need to help children feel they belong.

People to Please

The luckiest children are those who are raised by parents who are easy to please. These parents are quick to marvel at all those new questions, ideas, and creations. They enjoy their children. They love their children unconditionally. No ifs, ands, or buts. They love their children and they communicate this love.

An A wouldn't mean much to a six-year-old except for the fact that it makes dad happy. One plus one make two only because mom seems to approve of it. And when you went to your grandmother's for dinner, you ate more than usual because she told you, "It does my heart good to see you eat."

Easily pleased parents prove over and over again to their children that they can make their world a better place, that they can have an impact. Personal mastery gained in gradual yet consistent doses prepares children for a life where they can make a difference. In fact, one of our strongest and most basic drives is to have an impact. So strong is this desire believed to be that Erich Fromm insisted that people will either create and contribute *or* destroy. Either type of behavior leads to an observable effect on one's context.

Fromm said there can be no bystanders. Sitting on the sidelines doing nothing eventually becomes so uncomfortable that individuals will even choose destructiveness over impotence and complacency. Often the destructiveness is aimed at oneself. This is the internal, silent cancer of the soul that drains the spirit. We either grow or wither.

Fromm concluded that our natural preference is to grow into productive and caring beings who invest themselves in their own growth and the development of others. We are first and foremost creatures who prefer to build and create. We would like to make a positive impact. And this energy will flower if raised in the right context. The right context supports, respects, and encourages the natural inclinations of the child. When the environment appreciates a child's gifts—gifts that need to be given away—we find harmony. These are the arenas that produce healthy children.

As childhood gives way to the first signs of adulthood, a young person moves toward greater independence. Those easily pleased parents and grandparents are no longer waiting breathlessly for the results of each contest and challenge. But nature has prepared for this. All those voices that encourage the child become internalized. They find a home in one's heart and move in for a lifetime. The voices that said, "Atta boy," "You make me so proud," and "Thank you, that was very thoughtful" all lodge within. Once these voices are internalized, they can comment on just about everything. They provide thank-yous for all your thankless acts of kindness. Those who have internalized encouraging words remain capable of great compassion without needing applause. Gratitude is usually reinforcing, but if you will care for only those who can thank you, you will care only for a small fraction of humanity.

When I was a college student, I volunteered to work at a treatment center for severely emotionally disturbed children. While there, I learned much. At first, the most striking sight was the bizarre behavior of the kids. After a few weeks, however, I became just as interested in the behavior of the staff. During the course of any given day, staff members could be screamed at, spit on, bitten, or have things thrown at them. But they kept coming to work. Rarely did I ever hear a patient say "thank you." But the staff kept coming to work. Sometimes parents expressed gratitude; although that helped, it didn't explain why the staff kept coming to work.

In the years since this experience, I've seen hundreds of human-service professionals behave the same way. Remarkable people who go tremendous distances exerting incredible amounts of energy—all on a minimal amount of gratitude. It's not that they don't need gratitude. They do. It's just that certain people don't need it all the time. These special folks can tap rewards from within. Rewards that may have been placed there years before. As a result, they are able to help those who cannot say "thank you."

Children who live with easily pleased adults develop confidence in themselves. They learn that what they do can really mean something. Once this self-confidence begins to build, they move into a new stage of development. Children then ask themselves, "What will I do with my power?"

In their first attempts to answer this, kids look for role models to identify with. They try on different personalities and behaviors to see which, if any, fit. Within a brief period of time they can change their idols from musicians to athletes to movie-stars. This experimentation can begin in childhood and last well into adolescence. Eventually, however, we all feel pulled to decide what we will do with our lives.

When all this experimentation is through, the role models who exert the most influence over our lives and provide the clearest direction are precisely the same individuals whom we loved to please. The most powerful role models are those we have internalized. They stay with us, never going out of style or retiring. These heroes remain silent much of the time. No fanfare. No loud music. They stay with us as guides and provide a powerful influence on what we become.

Keep in mind that children do not learn kindness through words. They must see it. Then, when they begin to follow these examples, they need to see that *they* have the ability to contribute. They need to feel their powers and competence grow. Educators call this a sense of mastery. Beginning at an early age we need to know that we can affect our environment and help build the kind of world we would like to live in. We can never find comfort in the role of helpless victim.

The luckiest children are those who come in regular contact with adults who appreciate and empower them. Grownups such as these instill in children that sense of mastery needed to live healthy lives. This does not mean that structure and discipline are unnecessary. Children need to learn how to control their impulses. But we need to put more than "don'ts" in their consciences. We need to help them internalize voices that say, "Go ahead. You can do it. Do the right thing!" These are the voices of encouragement and they remind us that it's not enough to just stay out of trouble.

Hope

"Hope is the thing with feathers that perches in the soul, and sings the tune without the words, and never stops at all." These words written by Emily Dickinson seem to capture the essence of hope. She understood its power. She knew that once the soul accepts hope, however small the portion, it can never be erased completely. Children who acquire hope inherit a lifelong gift. Even glimpses of hope leave permanent rewards.

I have treated many adult survivors of child abuse and neglect. A high percentage of these people were the victims of severe maltreatment. Many have grown into troubled human beings unable to see much, if anything, worth living for. But what has been most surprising is the large number of abuse survivors who have managed to sustain a positive outook. In spite of all the pain that filled their early years, somehow arrows of optimism pierced their protective armor.

Most amazing, it seems clear that even brief encounters with kindness can have lasting effects. I have known many survivors of abuse and neglect who have grown into good, caring adults. People who have refused to carry with them and continue the cruelty they knew. Not long ago, psychiatrists began calling these special survivors "superkids" or "invulnerables." They become growing, productive prople even though raised in sometimes awful conditions.

Of the invulnerables I have known, all have had a similar experience. Amid all the pain, during a critical period of childhood, someone special came along and contradicted all else that life had taught them. Someone powerful enough to convince these superkids that goodness lives and can survive even the most difficult circumstances. These beacons of hope are often teachers who eventually become described in simple terms such as "the fourth-grade teacher who really believed in me." Usually this description is soon followed by the remark: "I'll never forget her."

These agents of hope can be scout leaders, coaches, clergy, or any adult who goes out of his or her way to improve the life of a child. They provide living proof that one person really can make a difference. We can't completely explain how brief exposures to caring can have such an impact on certain children. The fact remains, however, that they do. Small, strategically placed moments of caring can go a long way to reverse the tide of cruelty.

It has been said that children learn what they see. It has also been suggested by some that they learn what they hear. But more than anything, children learn what they *feel*. The lessons that last the longest are those that are felt the deepest.

Educators have identified what they call "teachable moments." During these "moments" the gates open and the child becomes susceptible to receiving new information. In theory, these opportunities don't last forever. They present themselves and then disappear. The best teachers may be thought of as those who help children arrive at teachable moments and then seize the chance to fill their minds.

We can use a similar concept to describe how children develop values like trust, caring, and hope. Even the most calloused and hardened individuals have *reachable moments*, times when they can be profoundly moved. In some people, including children, these moments are few and far between. But the invulnerables provide living proof that somehow certain arrows pierce even the thickest armor. Arrows that land at just the right instant.

If this is true, then there is no child without hope. Even children pulled from situations where they've known severe abuse and neglect. Even when the odds are long, some hope remains. During their reachable moments, children can feel the hope. Once they do, they begin the road to recovery.

Popular author and psychologist Bruno Bettelheim once wrote, "If a child is for some reason unable to imagine his future optimistically, arrest of development sets in." Bettelheim insisted that a lack of hope can lead to some of the most ravaging forms of mental illness such as autism where a child will completely withdraw into himself. A large part of mental health then becomes finding the belief that goodness exists and that everyone can make a significant contribution.

Bettelheim told the story of one child who plunged deeply into the pit of hopelessness. This youngster, however, received enough of the right kind of help to reverse her condition. "After prolonged therapy," wrote Bettelheim, she "emerged from her total autistic withdrawal and reflected on what characterizes good parents, she said: 'They hope for you.'"[1] Could it be that she returned from her journey within her psyche and soul with this astounding message? How could she have reached this conclusion? Deep within her illness, could she have found a reachable moment where this crucial lesson made its way to her? In any case, somehow she returned to our world with her cure. Like all children, she needed to *feel hope*.

Without hope children withdraw into themselves. Although only a few reach an autistic level, the others reach their own cellars. For the most part, we call these cellars selfishness and greed. If the world is unalterably wretched, we will spend our time looking out only for ourselves. But if the world can be a good, caring place, we will want to be a part of it.

Children develop a spirit that says "I can!" as long as they live in a place that says, "I will let you and I will help you!" Should hope wane, their reachable moments dwindle. Selfishness ensues and they are robbed of many of life's greatest pleasures. Should hope flourish, however, their lives become a steady series of reachable moments. They are easily touched, educated, and moved. They empathize and mobilize. They *feel* the need for their gifts and talents.

Fantasy

"Here's the first child we would like you to see," sighed the concerned principal. "Her name is Julie."

Julie was a nine-year-old with quite a history of emotional problems. She spent her days in a special classroom for behaviorally disordered (BD) students. Julie was, indeed, a special student within this special class. She had the looks of a little fashion model and the intellectual ability of children much older than she. "Hurricane Julie," as the teachers called her, was truly an exceptional child.

As fate would have it, Julie became my first client. Shortly after beginning my first graduate school internship, the powers that be handed me Julie. I don't think anyone thought she would let me get close enough to help her. But she certainly would be effective in breaking in a rookie therapist. When I first met Julie, it wasn't at all clear who had what to offer whom.

In the parlance of BD educators, Julie was a kicker. Prone to violent outbursts at the slightest provocation, Julie would kick anyone whom, at that moment, she considered a threat (which typically meant anyone in reach). This child's attacks were vicious and her intent clear. She meant to hurt.

Before I met her, a variety of treatment approaches were tried. A few appeared to work for a while but the short-term gains never lasted. At nine years old, Julie had already convinced some that she was heading toward becoming a "chronic"—someone who never gets better. The hope in her world was running out.

Besides her beauty and intelligence, Julie had two other traits that made her quite special. First, in spite of the fact that she could be a hellion to teachers, classmates, and older children, Julie was usually a remarkably loving child to younger children and youngsters with disabilities. In fact, she served diligently as their protector. Second, Julie possessed a marvelous ability to fantasize. Specifically, she would fantasize about wonderful, magical wedding ceremonies. These affairs represented the perfect world to her, where good people received their rewards and then lived happily ever after. When asked to tell her stories, Julie would put a spell on herself. These tales could settle and relax her even in the wake of some of her most violent outbursts.

One day her teacher tried to use Julie's fantasies to prevent future outbursts. What follows is the scene described to me by that teacher:

Teacher: Julie, how old are you?

Julie (immediately): Nine.

Teacher: And how old do you think you'll be when you get married?

Julie: Oh . . . twenty-five!

Teacher: Well, if you're going to get married, you're going to have to be nice to people. After all, no one will want to marry you if you're mean and nasty. Do you understand? Nobody wants to marry someone who kicks and screams. You're gonna have to be nice. If you want to have a beautiful wedding of your own, you're gonna have to be nice.

Julie (in a rage): For sixteen years?!?!

The teacher's point didn't make much sense to Julie. Asking Julie to control herself for sixteen years was like asking the ocean to stop making waves. Besides, Julie knew better than anyone that reality is reality and fantasy is fantasy. Also, being more sane than many had assumed, she knew that reverie could not correct all situations. As hard as she tried, she knew it did not change her realities. On the other hand, she also understood quite well the power contained in fantasy.

I met with Julie only twice. A few days after our second meeting, her family moved. I've never learned what became of her. I guess I'll never know. From the pieces I could put together, however, some theories emerge.

All the evidence available suggested that Julie was an abused child. At the very least, she was probably exposed to violence in her home. As a result, she carried much anger within her and, to make matters worse, she was unable to develop adequate impulse controls to corral her hostility. When her parents learned she was seeing a therapist at school, I believe they transferred her to protect the secret of whatever was going on at home. It appeared that Julie would never get the treatment she needed.

In spite of what was a grim outlook for this child, there is reason to hope that she survived and possibly even prospered. Somehow this small wonder found a way to hold on to hope. Through fantasy she could control her torment. It helped her keep some faith in the world and the people in it. While she was too powerless to improve her situation, she clung to the belief that things, no matter how bad they became, could get better. My hope is that Julie held on to this belief until she developed the power to change her life.

Some psychiatrists might call Julie a successful schizophrenic. She used a vivid fantasy world to help navigate the troubled waters of her everyday life. We could say that the crazy part of her sustained a hope that better things could happen.

We could make an argument that all happy, healthy children are successful schizophrenics. They transcend their relative powerlessness with dreams of futures with incredible powers and accomplishments. Healthy children naturally dream the impossible dream. They see themselves becoming doers, contributors, and achievers. They believe they will have a significant impact on the world even when their present conditions might indicate quite the opposite.

Kind people live with a special fantasy. Somewhere deep inside they know their simple acts of concern are really wonderful opportunities to improve the world. Kindness is fantastic (i.e., fantasy-like). It has a quixotic element to it. Like Don Quixote—a very simple man himself—kind people may be tilting at windmills. Maybe they overestimate the need for their compassion. Maybe they're naive to sacrifice anything in their efforts to care. Or perhaps they know something others don't. Something that wouldn't make sense to unkind people.

This may be another reason why altruistic souls are reluctant to talk about their motives. Could it be that they believe that their explanations might not make sense?

Fantasy seems to be a friend of kindness. Your kindness doesn't have to make sense. Truly compassionate people tend to be impossible dreamers. They can see and feel a gentler, more giving world. They can almost touch it.

Once children envision this place, they begin building it.

Discouraged

Children need to know how far they can venture before it starts becoming dangerous. Ideally, as their skills build, they feel more confident in a wider variety of contexts. If everything works the way it should, children gradually make friends with the world.

Contrary to what seems to be common knowledge, children are not inherently selfish. Instead, they possess an inherent desire to share. And this drive will grow abundantly in friendly soil. This is not to say that healthy children will give away all their food and clothes. They know that certain items need to be kept. It can be tough to determine what needs to stay and what can go. Children struggle with the monumental task of finding out: "How can I take care of me *and* take care of you?" Those fortunate enough to find this balance reach a state that we often call mental health but may best be described as harmony. This is the place where the "pieces" seem to come together.

The road to harmony runs into extremes in both directions. Complete and utter selfishness gives way to emptying the toy box for a needier child. Then, before anyone can begin to explain the sudden saintliness, stinginess returns. Hopefully, the road eventually straightens. The wild swings reach a compromise and we come to understand that loving ourselves and loving others are virtually one and the same. One cannot exist without the other.

Scientists are now coming to understand that young children, even infants, are capable of empathy. They can feel the pain of others. This empathy calls for a desire to help those in need. In spite of their bouts of selfishness, children are, on the whole, tremendously caring and giving creatures. They feel the distress of others and they want to have an impact. These two qualities mix to produce altruism.

With empathy and the desire to contribute already in place early in life, children really lack only one ingredient necessary to make significant improvements in their contexts—power. Children are not going to make the planet safe for democracy. They aren't the ones to discover the cure for cancer. As children, they won't find a way to stop child abuse or racism. Their contributions are small. They share their things. They give hugs and say "I love you" without provocation. They protect younger kids and, usually, try not to hurt your feelings. And they keep coming back when you've hurt theirs. I've never met a child who didn't want to be a good person. I've met many, I'm sad to say, who have stopped believing that they could ever achieve such a noble goal.

What happens to the simple kindness so apparent in child-hood? Why don't grownups give each other their drawings or make up right after a big quarrel? Why do adults have to think so hard about how to approach someone in pain while even two-year-olds will spontaneously reach out and walk toward someone who's hurting? Where does the kindness go?

To help us answer this, we have at least one crucial clue. That clue is this. Certain research has pointed out that generosity and other forms of altruistic behavior increase with age, *until preadolescence.*[2] Then things begin to change. As children move toward adolescence, many lose the compassion they once knew. They become self-absorbed as they move into the "real world."

This shouldn't be too surprising. The fact is, generosity can be frightening to parents. They know how overwhelming a force it can be. Left unrepressed, generosity can become a way of life. So children learn that it's O.K. to give way their art but it's not all right to give away their money. The message: don't give away objects that are or can be useful. These are meant to be kept.

Parents who discourage charity usually do so with all the best intentions. They want to protect their children. In a dog-eat-dog world, the good guys finish last. Besides, there may not be a real future in helping unfortunates. Indeed, we have to ask ourselves, "Why would parents want their children to be kind? Why would parents encourage their children to sacrifice for some greater good?" The answer, I believe, is almost too simple to comprehend. Only parents who have learned to feel kindness will be willing or able to teach kindness. These are the parents who will pass it on to the next generation.

Parents, however, whose focus is to protect what they have, will in turn pass this orientation on to their charges. In these families, not only is altruism not reinforced, it may also be mocked and ridiculed. Children then become ashamed of their natural desire to make things better. Once a child becomes ashamed of his need to be kind bitterness sets in. Bitterness that can last a lifetime.

It makes sense to prepare young people for the realities they will face. But first we ought to examine how real our realities are. Maybe we are preparing children for a real world that doesn't exist. If life were as rigid, competitive, and cruel as I'm told it is in the real world, we would all be selfish and miserable. This doesn't seem to be the case.

It might be more correct to suggest that our children face a world filled with repressed caring. A world with millions and millions of people bursting at the seams to start a more loving, compassionate lifestyle. People just starving for the courage to release this force. Ironically, most of these folks believe they are the only ones who feel this way. They were taught that the *real* Golden Rule says: look out for yourself. So they feel alone and ashamed because of their secret desire to be conspicuously loving souls.

Preparing young people for this tragic myth we call the real world can kill their spirit. It requires that they leave much too much of themselves at the door to adulthood. It insists that they abandon the qualities that would bring them self-acceptance and contentment.

We are much wiser to prepare them for the *ideal world*, the place that welcomes their healthiest traits, the place that appreciates their contributions, the place where they feel they belong.

And even if, after all their preparation, they cannot find this world, they will be prepared for the most honorable endeavor in life—building it.

The Chamber of Convictions

Deep inside us there is a small room with a strong lock on its sturdy door. This is where we keep our most important lessons. These lessons compose our essence, our core, our most basic and permanent values. Beliefs stored in this chamber are well protected. They orient us. Whenever we become too confused we can return to these lessons to be reminded of what's important.

This chamber is quite small. Only the most essential beliefs are afforded this special protection. Once secure in these quarters, ideas grow roots deep and strong. The contents of the chamber provide the basics, the foundation of our identity. No matter what happens or how muddled life becomes, the Chamber of Convictions provides the security of knowing that some guidelines remain virtually constant.

Hopefully, the Chamber of Convictions becomes filled with healthy values. But we must understand that this is not always the case. Many individuals fill their Chamber with irrational and destructive beliefs. Examples of these ruinous ideas are: I deserve to be hurt. Only fools let down their guard. Don't trust anyone. Everyone is better than me. It's not hard to see how painful life can be if we rely on these terrible notions to guide us.

Once a belief enters the Chamber of Convictions it is protected from compromise. A belief does not enter the Chamber until it has become a conviction. Only when a person has decided that a particular resolution is so important that it should never be altered will it enter the Chamber. There it is intended to be held and protected forever.

Material stored in the Chamber can, however, be changed. But this change does not come easily. We have to accept the fact that once an idea enters the Chamber, it will resist change. This warning will suffice for now. We will return to this tremendously significant issue in chapter 7 when we deal with transformations.

All we need to understand here is that when a belief, or a set of beliefs, enters the Chamber, it will likely become a guide that remains operative throughout one's life. The most immediate implication of this is that we cannot overestimate the power of lessons learned during childhood. The Chamber fills early. With this in mind, we can begin to understand how children develop the convictions to become caring, compassionate, and generous.

Convictions tend to be passed through the generations. Just about all the evidence accumulated to date supports the position that children begin learning altruism through role models. One important study concluded that "the optimal condition for the development of sympathetic helpful behavior was one in which children observed an adult manifesting altruism at every level—in principle and in practice, both toward the child and toward others."[3] Another significant study found that "the weight of the evidence clearly indicates that children are likely to imitate the altruistic actions of models they observe and thus enhance their own prosocial behavior. Even relatively brief exposures to a generous model may have some generalized and lasting positive effects."[4]

Children learn what they see and hear but, more than anything, *they learn what they feel*. They are more likely to hold on to lessons they can feel. In order to put something deep inside themselves—all the way down to the Chamber of Convictions—they must feel it. This is the route lessons must travel in order to be lasting.

In a fascinating study, Professors Samuel and Pearl Oliner examined the personality traits of those individuals who risked their lives to rescue Jews from the Nazis during World War II. These rescuers knew they would be sent to concentration camps or executed if they were caught harboring Jews. Yet thousands of brave souls carried on this heroic work.

In their book *The Altruistic Personality*, the Oliners sought to explain their findings. "What distinguished rescuers was not their lack of concern with self, external approval, or achievement," they wrote, "but rather their capacity for extensive relationships—their stronger sense of attachment to others and their feeling of responsibility for the welfare of others, including those outside their immediate familial or communal circles."[5]

The Oliners also addressed the childhoods of these rescuers. During the course of their research, they found significant differences between the families that produced rescuers and those that produced nonrescuers. They provided a composite portrait of the families that raised those who would become rescuers.

> It begins in close family relationships in which parents model caring behavior and communicate values. . . . [There exists] a heavy dose of reasoning—explanations of why behaviors are inappropriate, often with reference to their consequences for others. Physical punishment is rare; when used, it tends to be a singular event rather than routine. . . . Simultaneously, however, parents set high standards they expect their children to meet, particularly with regard to caring for others. They implicitly or explicitly communicate the obligation to help others in a spirit of generosity, without concern for external rewards or reciprocity. . . . Dependability, responsibility, and self-reliance are valued because they facilitate taking care of oneself and others.[6]

Children who live in an environment where they *feel* kindness will learn kindness. Compassion will enter the Chamber of Convictions where it will build a force of its own. Once this begins, caring behavior will sustain itself with or without rewards. As in the case of rescuers during the Holocaust, it can even sustain itself through the most oppressive circumstances. With strong roots, the Kindness Vine can survive the most difficult times.

Children inherit the kindness of others. They internalize the kindness they experience. Once they have internalized the conviction that caring for others is the right way to live, external rewards are no longer necessary. Once this conviction has entered the Chamber, gold stars and public recognition are no longer needed to perpetuate compassion. It exists simply because it is the right thing to do.

It would be a mistake, though, to say that generosity lacks rewards. Many healthy traits and positive qualities accompany a caring lifestyle. If we look at all the research done in this area, we find a fairly consistent result. Compared with their peers, especially generous and caring children (or as some psychologists say, "children with strong prosocial dispositions") appear to be better adjusted, socially skilled, more expressive, more gregarious, and somewhat assertive.[7] They don't finish last. Far from it.

In order for children to build a conviction that they want to be good, caring people, they need at least two things. First, they seem to need effective role models who demonstrate what compassion is and what it can do. They need to spend time with adults who value kindness. Second, children need opportunities to act in caring ways. They need to feel kindness. With each act, they strengthen their self-respect and their identities as caring people.

A growing number of educators and psychologists recommend that children be put in situations where they can help others. Experiences such as caring for pets, keeping watch over younger siblings, and tutoring other children can help tremendously.[8] These activities help develop a self-concept and ultimately a conviction that says, "I care!"

Once kindness becomes a conviction in children, these young people become the ones who set the examples. They start the waves. They become branches of the Kindness Vine.

3

GETTING WARM

Commit random gestures of kindness,
perform senseless acts of beauty.
Anonymous

Once upon a time in the village of Sea Isle, there lived a man named Bonner who gave kindness to people. He put it in simple yet finely crafted small leather boxes, each one a little different than all the others, and each created with a great deal of love by this gentleman who hummed while he worked. He gave the boxes, free of charge, to anyone who wanted one. And the people of Sea Isle were the kindest in the land.

One day two scoundrels arrived in the village and quickly learned about Bonner and his boxes of kindness. They soon convinced Bonner that people in other towns sorely needed kindness and that it was only right that he provide boxes for these unfortunate souls.

Being a generous man, Bonner began producing more boxes than ever before. He trusted the two strangers and told them how to give the boxes in such a way as to maximize the kindness within. The rogues agreed completely and then set off with a cartful of Bonner's finest work.

The scoundrels, however, did not do as Bonner had instructed. Instead, they traveled hurriedly to the town of Emtee where they sold the boxes to the highest bidders. They told the unsuspecting people of Emtee that if they purchased the boxes, they would be forever blessed with kindness and happiness. They also insisted that the more boxes one bought, the happier one would be.

Soon the boxes showed up all over town. People were flaunting them on their carriages, their doorways, and even on their hats.

Back in Sea Isle, the people understood that there were fewer boxes available to them because so many were sent elsewhere. It was a sacrifice they gladly made.

Before long, the people of Emtee realized they had been duped. No one had become kinder or happier. But by now the scoundrels had fled with their profits. Seeing no one else to blame, they called for Bonner to stand trial for fraud and deceit.

Although hardly a wealthy man, Bonner used all his savings to buy back the boxes. He then went to the town dump where he found many other boxes that had been discarded by disenchanted owners.

He walked his cart back to Sea Isle where he distributed the boxes just as he always had.

And the people of Sea Isle lived happily ever after as the kindest people in the land.

Stories

I've heard it said that God creates so many people because He loves stories. While I suspect there is more to it than this, the point is well taken. We are all natural-born story creators and storytellers. We produce and collect stories, call them memories, and carry them with us as our personal histories.

I wouldn't be surprised if God's favorite stories are tales of kindness. I can't prove this, you know, but it seems like a possibility. In fact, I wonder if people would feel closer to God if they told Him more about the kindness they saw in the world. Furthermore, creating and collecting anecdotes about charity may keep you far from the devil. I can't imagine that he can stomach much in the way of caring.

Besides the spiritual rewards, there are also psychological benefits to compassion. Few things raise your self-esteem more than knowing you've helped someone. And receiving kindness from others can sustain your faith in humanity. If we keep these events in our memories, our view of the world will never become too bleak.

I remember one bitter cold January morning when my car broke down while I was driving across Indiana. As the car coughed to a stop, the first thought that crossed my mind was, "I don't know a single person in this entire state!" Several minutes later an old rusted car pulled up behind me and a man dressed in ragged clothes got out. For an instant, I thought he was going to rob me. Instead, this soul without gloves fixed my car. As he turned to leave, I reached into my pocket to give him some money. But he refused to accept it. Instead, he shook my hand, gave me one of the most memorable smiles I have ever seen, and drove off (back to heaven perhaps).

As my car and I warmed up again, it occurred to me how valuable a story this man had just given me. To fully appreciate the impact of this act maybe you have to know what it's like to be lost and freezing. In any case, I think I began writing this book as I sat there thawing out. This man in patched clothes did much more than start my car. He started me looking for and listening to stories of kindness.

An act of caring can pass in seconds but the memory—the story—lasts forever. Holding on to these stories can be very healthy. Stories have a way of multiplying. Once you start holding on to a few, others appear. Stories tend to come to those who appreciate them. And if one cannot find kindness, one can always create it. Stories of kindness are there for everyone.

We learn compassion by holding on to our stories. The most powerful tales seem to be those we have experienced firsthand. We are more likely to become caring people if we have come to feel kindness. Still, one can be moved by others' stories. Especially if one has developed the gift of empathy.

Empathy

"One learns peoples through the heart, not the eyes or the intellect," wrote Mark Twain. An important lesson, that. Twain must have known quite a bit about people. It might seem that we come to know human beings by figuring out their stimuli and responses, their instincts, drives, and reinforcers. And if we could measure all the psychological dimensions that we are told are so important, we would know all there is to know about a particular individual. But as Twain pointed out, this is not the case. In order to *know people* we have to develop a feel for them. This means we must first learn to empathize.

It's more or less a natural reaction for mothers to start shivering when they find their children are cold. Mothers can empathize so strongly with their children that they feel the fear that comes with a nightmare or the embarrassment that accompanies wetting the bed or the elation that arises at Christmastime. Mothers have a knack for feeling their children's feelings. We call this the power of empathy.

Healthy mothers empathize with their children. They feel their pain and their happiness. Children also can, to some extent, empathize with people closest to them. Even babies possess a natural, yet undeveloped, ability to sense the feelings of certain others. Should this fragile sense grow and mature, these children will grow into adults capable of being wonderful parents to a new generation.

Psychologist Carolyn Zahn-Waxler of the National Institute of Mental Health defines empathy as, at its most basic level, a "participation in the feelings and ideas of others." It involves an emotional joining in another person's experience.[1] Empathy may be our sixth sense. With it we come to know a sensational world—the world of feelings. With this gift we can understand more than we could using all our other senses. With it we enter the marvelous world of other people. Empathy is the vehicle that lifts us off our own small isolated domain and into a universe of millions of fascinating planets.

With empathy, our stories come alive. We can know the characters that enter our lives and we can realize the impact they have on us. Empathy allows us to feel the core of humanity that runs through us all. It also gives us an understanding of and an appreciation for the individuality and uniqueness of those who share our lives. We then feel a connection with those who may look and sound very different than ourselves. When we feel this connection, we become capable of great compassion.

Sometimes it's the little things that spark empathy. Even in wartime, events occur that cause enemies to see their relatedness. André Malraux wrote that you cannot aim a flamethrower at someone who is looking at you. George Orwell described his inability to shoot at an enemy soldier whose pants were falling down: "A man who is holding up his trousers isn't a 'Fascist,' he is visibly a fellow creature, similar to yourself, and you don't feel like shooting at him."[2] When we can feel our connection, we lose our hostility. There are no enemies among those on the same Vine.

Cruelty survives only as long as we fail to attach or connect with our foe. We (i.e., humans) give our enemies dehumanizing names to help blind us to their humanity. We can aim our weapons at gooks, ragheads, spics, crackers, and niggers. But fingers begin to twitch and consciences start to growl when, through the sights, we see fellow human beings. It's harder to hurt someone who we feel is a part of us.

In an article appearing in the prestigious journal *American Psychologist,* researcher C. Daniel Batson made an extensive review of the literature available on the human capacity for caring. Afterward, he reached this conclusion: "All the research I have mentioned suggests that our capacity for altruistic caring is limited to those for whom we feel empathy."[3] In other words, empathy precedes genuine kindness.

It's true that we can behave in a caring manner for other reasons. John may help someone he cares little for if he is paid for doing so. But in this case, his altruism will stop when the payment ceases. (Unless, of course, his mercenary act of altruism stirred within him a feeling of empathy for the person he assisted.) Genuine caring, however, begins with empathy. The feeling initiates the act.

Sometimes we have to get closer to people to empathize with them. Sometimes we need to see our reflection in their eyes. One of the first signs of empathy is the emerging sense that you and I are *we*. That somehow, even though appearances may suggest otherwise, we belong to the same tribe. A tribe that has a language in common, the language of human feelings. The more feelings we allow to live inside us, the greater our vocabulary. Someone with a large vocabulary has the ability and the sensitivity to connect with virtually anyone.

Carl Rogers used to say that the feeling of being truly understood is very similar to the feeling of being loved. One cannot help but be moved by the profound sense that comes with the realization that another human being really understands and accepts you. I'm afraid that many, many people go through their entire lives without ever having this experience. Without ever having been loved or understood, a person tends to become isolated and withdrawn, often feeling too much of his or her own pain to reach out and empathize with another. This isolation can lead to a destructiveness that focuses on oneself, others, or both.

The remedy for this condition involves, first and foremost, finding someone who might understand. We put ourselves back together as we begin to reattach ourselves to others. As psychiatrist Frederic Flach suggests, "There is perhaps no more effective way to relieve psychic pain than to be in contact with another human being who understands what you are going through and can communicate such understanding to you."[4] In his book *Resilience,* Flach goes on to make a most interesting point. He reminds his readers that "you will have to keep in mind that there are no perfect empathizers; one friend may understand certain aspects of your life that others won't."[5] We can jump to the conclusion "no one understands me" much too soon. We can give up hope when we should be looking for the person or people capable of empathizing with us. This is why people so often change their circle of friends after a crisis. We sometimes find that our old circle of friends cannot understand what we've been through. We then must look for folks who, perhaps because they've been down the same path, can comprehend what we are experiencing.

This, in fact, is one of the most remarkable consequences of tragedy. If we survive and then find the courage to keep the experience in our memories, we will greatly increase our power to empathize. In many ways, the most courageous among us are those who survive their tragedies and go on with their lives without forgetting or denying their tragic experience. Tragedy can cultivate our powers of empathy. If we remember all those horrible feelings, our emotional vocabulary grows and we can relate to a much wider group of people.

One of the ironies of tragedy is the reality that it leaves many people isolated and alone while others who have weathered the same storm become much closer to the rest of humanity than they have ever been. There are probably several reasons for this, but I believe that one of the most important differences between these groups involves empathy. Tragedy can cultivate empathy. When this occurs, people survive their holocausts with a stronger sense of purpose in their lives. More than anything, should empathy grow, survivors emerge with a greater sense of connectedness to the rest of the universe.

As empathy builds, so does its ability to cover long distances. Empathic beings hurt when they read in the newspaper how parents on the other side of the globe are desperately searching for their missing child. They feel the fear and uncertainty when they hear the news anchor describe the plight of someone waiting for a donor to provide a needed organ transplant. We can participate in the emotions of people we will never meet.

Empathy joins people. At times we can do little more than empathize. Even at these times empathy has its rewards. It connects us with humankind and this provides contentment and security. Frequently, empathy is followed by kindness. Empathy allows us to feel the need for compassion. Once this feeling comes to us, we look for the courage to act. Empathy and courage produce many great acts of kindness.

Not many incidents torment the soul more than feeling someone's pain but not moving to help because of fear. Empathy without courage leads to feelings of guilt and cowardice. You hear the call but are afraid to answer. You feel the pull but are too scared to move. So you sit there or walk away knowing—at least at some level—that you were not true to yourself, that you moved away from what you knew was right. The cowardice can gnaw at you. It can lodge in your conscience like a thorn. If too many thorns accumulate, you may lose your ability to empathize. You will be too involved with your own pain to feel that of others.

Empathy is a gift that brings with it a grave responsibility. Our spirit will not let us avoid what we feel and our conscience will not ignore what we know is wrong. Without a doubt, there are times when the greatest burden we can carry is the gift of empathy. Life might be easier for us if, when we saw someone in need, we could just turn away without a single twinge. Then we could choose whom to feel for. Because, with empathy, it seems we are chosen by fate to do something that might involve great sacrifice. As Batson reports,

Indeed, often it seems that we must take steps to avoid feeling empathy, whether for the homeless, those starving in Africa and Cambodia, or refugees in Central America. Lest we feel too much, we turn the corner, switch channels, flip the page, or think of something else. Could this apparent necessity to defend ourselves against empathy be a clue to the magnitude of our capacity to care?[6]

With empathy we not only see the need, we *feel* it. We can try to repress our empathy because we are aware of our tremendous capacity to care. If we don't see the need, we won't be pulled to fill it. But if we do see the need, well . . .

The kindest people around have a special sensitivity to the needs of others. But in order to develop this sensitivity, we must become vulnerable. We must be willing to allow someone else's suffering into our hearts. We must be willing to feel their pain. Empathy is a wonderful gift but it comes with a price—vulnerability. People who allow themselves to feel also allow themselves to be hurt.

There are times in everyone's life when we have a special need for kindness. These are often the times when we are hurt. During these periods, compassion can restore our faith in the healing process. If we know we can heal, we are more likely to risk being hurt. We then allow ourselves the vulnerability that comes with opening ourselves to the needs and feelings of another.

There are other times when an encounter with kindness can work miracles. When someone is ready to learn something important, a small sign of caring can have a lasting impact. Similarly, when someone has reached a point where he or she is deciding about the value of humanity or the nature of life itself, a simple act of charity can restore life to a cynical soul. Often it is not the size of the good deed that counts but rather the timing.

As Frederic Flach pointed out, there are no perfect empathizers. We cannot always know when someone is in need of kindness. Some have developed their sensitivities more than others, but no one owns a patent on this gift. But every act of kindness increases the likelihood that compassion will find its way to those who need it.

The Calling

We have already discussed the fact that much, perhaps most, of the research coming out of biology and psychology has concluded that genuine altruism does not exist. The sciences have decided, for the most part, that we really only *appear* to be caring when in fact we will act compassionately only if we are rewarded for doing so. According to this view, I will not be benevolent toward a friend unless I will profit from my action. Ultimately, so the theory goes, all behavior is rooted in either self-preservation or self-gratification. Consequently, there are no truly selfless acts.

Albert Einstein claimed, "Your theory will determine what you see." In other words, if I believe that all behavior is basically selfish, I will see selfishness everywhere. The person who donates blood to the Red Cross will be doing so to get people to approve of him. People who volunteer their time in nursing homes only want to feel holier than thou. And those who diligently search for a missing child are merely interested in the publicity and appreciation they will receive if they find the lost youngster. Everyone is after something.

We have a talent for seeing selfishness. All we have to do is assume it is there and it appears. If we believe it is everywhere, then we live in a very selfish world. A world where we would have to spend our time protecting ourselves because if everyone is out for themselves, then there can be no trust. Selfishness can be more contagious than kindness. It spreads through our minds and then through our worlds.

Science has always had a difficult time understanding compassion. It doesn't fit into precise equations. It can vanish in contexts that look ideal and then reappear in the most unlikely places. Churchgoers can honk their horns and squabble over a space at the church parking lot, and yet acts of great sacrifice and caring were performed in the concentration camps. Kindness seems to be influenced, even guided, by forces not well understood by the sciences.

The funny thing about kindness is that you have to believe it in order to see it. If you don't, you won't. At the very least you have to be prepared to believe that there may be such a thing as honest, selfless compassion. Then, and only then, will the colors of kindness begin to appear.

One of the primary reasons we are so ready to see selfishness is that we can explain it. Concepts like self-preservation and taking care of number one can make sense. Self-gratification can seem quite natural, and to some extent it probably is. Protecting, feeding, and entertaining ourselves are such obvious drives that they really need little explanation. They are so apparent that they are easy to believe. Even when we are pressed to examine these drives we, as a culture, tend to fall back on the worn line, "It's our animal nature."

We're pretty sure about our animal nature. It's our human nature that confuses us. It can be difficult to explain, especially if we try to explain human nature with terms that really apply only to our animal nature. Within our animal nature we behave for the rewards. Within our human nature we also act for rewards. But our animal reward is very different from our higher, more human rewards. In fact, they are almost opposites. To say that all human behavior is shaped by rewards tells us little about people. We need to know more about how we come to act the way we do. We seem to have a grasp on selfishness (part of our "animal nature"); now we need to develop a better understanding of caring (part of our "human nature").

For our purposes we need to specifically address the question, "Why kindness?" Right or wrong, many people will not believe in kindness until they answer this. Others may believe but are reluctant to participate in something they don't understand. And although we will never completely articulate the reasons compassion exists, we can at least begin to put the answer to "Why kindness?" into words.

We start by moving out of the biological and psychological realm and into the spiritual world. In the spiritual world, "reward" has a new meaning, a meaning hard to define yet, in its own way, understandable. Caring benefits everyone involved, but it benefits the caretaker in a special way. It has an extraordinary effect.

In *The Prophet*, Kahlil Gibran wrote this about friendship: "And let there be no purpose in friendship save the deepening of the spirit." This is the best description I have ever encountered of the rewards of friendship and also the *rewards of kindness*. The *deepening of the spirit*. We can't measure this. Without a special sensitivity, we may not even feel it. A certain feeling comes as the spirit deepens. It is the sensation we experience when we know we are doing (or have done) the right thing. It also arises in the face of uncertainty when we try something that we believe (but are not sure) is the correct path.

Psychology might explain this sensation as a consequence of following one's conscience. A happy conscience purrs. No guilt. No need to punish oneself for transgressions. A peaceful conscience reminds you, "You haven't done anything wrong." We enjoy knowing this. An angry conscience can be a terrible companion, constantly rumbling after it has been violated. But a serene conscience dwells blissfully, silently in the psyche. No static. No noise. Cooperating with our consciences can help quite a bit in the pursuit of mental health. Without the distractions of a dissatisfied conscience, we can focus on our work, our relationships, and our play.

With many descriptions of the human condition, the story ends here. A guilt-free existence is often considered the epitome of emotional health and happiness. But these stories are misleading. It's not enough to say, "I didn't do anything wrong." In order to find meaning and contentment, we must do more than quiet the conscience. We must fulfill our callings.

In some ways, a calling is to the spiritual realm what a conscience is to the psychological. But whereas a conscience is filled with "don'ts" (e.g., don't eat too much; you'll get worms.), a calling is a collection of "dos" (e.g., do the right thing!). People led to believe that a silent conscience leads to a happy life frequently come to doubt what they have been taught. Sometimes they look for the guilt that must be there (they think) to explain their discontent. *They look for sins when they should be looking for signs*, signs of what they are called to do. No one ever reached their potential solely by pacifying their conscience. There is more to health and happiness than obeying the "don'ts." We have to listen to the "dos."

Our callings are a part of our spiritual dimension. This realm operates differently than the physical and psychological dimensions. In the physical and psychological levels of our being, rewards are things that we receive. In the spiritual arena, we are rewarded by what we give. We are called to give and each time we do, we feel a deepening of the spirit.

Giving is the common denominator that runs through everyone's calling. Once we acknowledge our spiritual dimension, we soon come to realize that we are giving creatures and that being fulfilled as human beings means contributing to the welfare of the universe. The spirit is rewarded with the opportunity to give. Because these opportunities are endless, our spirit has an unlimited potential for growth. If we seize these opportunities, we move toward spiritual health.

In my book *Facing Fear: The Search for Courage,* I described the search for our callings as similar to the children's game "Warmer-Colder." As we move in the direction of our calling, we become warmer, more contented and compassionate. But if we move away from our callings, we become cold, cynical, and selfish. We are where we belong when we follow our callings. This path brings out the best in us.

All of our callings have something important in common: they all involve giving of ourselves. We are all called to use our gifts in the service of humanity. Furthermore, we are all called to serve in our own unique ways. Humankind has many needs, and it takes many talents to fill them.

"If a man is called to be a streetsweeper," said Martin Luther King, "he should sweep streets even as Michelangelo painted, or Beethoven composed music, or Shakespeare wrote poetry. He should sweep streets so well that all the hosts of heaven and earth will pause to say, here lived a great streetsweeper who did his job well." In the final analysis, there may be little difference between the contributions of, say, Shakespeare and this great streetsweeper. They are equally successful to the extent that they have each made valiant and honest efforts to answer their callings.

Our callings continue throughout our lives. They may remain fairly constant or make rather sudden changes that pull us into new, sometimes frightening, directions. Although it is sometimes difficult to hear the call, it is always there. Richard Bach, author of *Jonathan Livingston Seagull*, said it well when he realized: "Here's a test to find whether your mission on earth is finished: If you are alive, it isn't." Even when your path seems to disappear, it continues.

You cannot, nor should you feel required to, cure all the world's hurts. We live in a world with countless needs, and yet we each have limited resources. Still, as part of our callings, we possess special sensitivities to particular needs. Some of us are drawn to children in need, others to victims of injustice. Some of us feel pulled to the plight of the homeless while others own a heightened awareness of the pain of physical illness. There's a kind of suffering that touches all of us, if we let it. The pain that reaches you most deeply represents a part of your calling.

The warmness that arises within us as we follow our callings brings us closer to people. One of the consequences of this closeness is that we can feel another's pain. If we let people touch us, we can be hurt. But avoiding our call to contribute does not improve our lives. Without a calling, our lives would lack meaning and direction. In *The Divine Comedy* Dante wrote, "In the middle of the journey of our life, I found myself in a dark wood, for I had lost the right path." The right path also has its share of sorrows. It is still a far better place to be than the "dark wood."

Not long ago, in a small restaurant, I saw two exceptional beings shuffle along their paths together. As I sat eating with a friend, I watched an old man and a young man walk toward the door. The old man was weak and relied on the young man's arms for much needed support. He kept his eyes on the door and directed the twosome. The young man had Down's syndrome. As he supported his companion, his eyes wandered around soaking up the scenery. They seemed to fit together.

Before they managed to leave the restaurant, the young man looked to me. When our eyes met, he held his glance. He didn't utter a word but I sensed him saying, "Do you see us?" I did. And I could not help but be moved by this walking lesson in life.

It would be hard for either of these two gentlemen to find their way alone. Together, though, they could not only survive but have quite an impact on anyone who might notice them. They demonstrated a powerful message. We need to match gifts with needs.

We all face certain questions. Which opportunities are my opportunities? Of all the invitations to contribute, which are the ones that affect me most profoundly? We answer these questions with our lives and how we live them. Being touched is a part of being called. The people and events that move us start us toward answering our call. I believe that callings come from God, but we all need to decide this for ourselves. We need to reach our own conclusions. The only way to find out where the calling is coming from is to follow it.

Empathy and the Calling

Callings come to people in different ways. We can hear them in our dreams or they can whisper during times of quiet reflection. We can hear them in solitude or in the midst of a roaring crowd. They can come in the form of a sudden awakening or gradually over the course of years. A calling can be a scream and it can be spoken in sign language. Callings can be felt in our hearts and understood in our minds. We can accept them peacefully or spend our lives fighting them.

With all this in mind, we will now consider one particular way of receiving a calling—through other people. People are capable of bringing our callings to us. I don't think they do so deliberately as often as they do it spontaneously. If we allow ourselves to understand other people (i.e., empathize), we may get a much clearer sense of our mission. Without empathy, however, we cut ourselves off from important sources. This leads to bitterness and a loss of direction. Without a connection to the rest of humanity, life becomes meaningless.

Those who plug into the feelings and needs of people are much more likely to find their path. Take Henri Landwirth for instance. As a teenager, he spent five years in Nazi concentration camps. During these years he was surrounded by other young people who, like himself, lived in the face of death. Both of his parents were killed by the Nazis. Yet in spite of the horror, hardships, and misery, Mr. Landwirth avoided the bitterness and even (miraculously) found gratitude. He was thankful that his life had been spared and his thankfulness has never left him. Mr. Landwirth became the founder of a special vacation village for terminally ill children called Give Kids the World. The village is designed for dying children whose last wish is to visit Disneyland, Sea World, or any of the other attractions in central Florida. All the children need to do is ask and Mr. Landwirth's organization will arrange to bring the child and his or her family to Give Kids the World. In short, it's an all-out effort to fulfill final dreams.

"This is my life now," says Henri Landwirth. "I'm fulfilling a spiritual need. . . . This is more rewarding than anything I've ever done."[7] We fulfill our own spiritual needs by helping others fill theirs. The spirit is rewarded, and thus enhanced, through giving. If we feel the needs of others, we are likely to find a mission "more rewarding than anything."

There is also another side to this. One that might not be obvious. Just as we can realize our callings by connecting with people, we can ourselves carry a calling to others. This may be accomplished in numerous ways. Whenever we point out talents in someone, we may be helping them find their purpose in life. Parents and teachers frequently have these opportunities. Whenever we take the time to listen to someone long enough and carefully enough to help them sort out their priorities, we help them find direction. Providing others with new stories and fresh experiences also opens them to new messages. We can encourage folks to listen for their callings.

Maybe it would be more correct to suggest that people bring us *pieces* of our callings. Like the pieces to a puzzle, as we understand the relationship among them, we begin to see the picture. It's a bit humbling and, at the same time, empowering to think of ourselves as a piece of someone else's calling. The size of the pieces seem to vary, some large, some small, but all necessary. Some of us do a better job of carrying a calling than others. Some are truly exceptional calling carriers. They are so honest and unpretentious that the messages they carry come through simply yet powerfully. They have a way of moving people.

Then there are those of us too bitter or too protected to communicate any part of a calling to anyone. For example, consider a seventeen-year-old young man I know whom I will call Jeremy. If you listen to Jeremy for a while, you might think that he never met a person he didn't hate. He shows the world little more than contempt. In his settled moments, Jeremy will articulate quite well a desire to be separated from everyone. He says relationships inevitably lead to pain and that he has been hurt enough. So no more pain.

As I write this, Jeremy is enrolled in a chemical-dependency program for teenagers. For several years he has been addicted to alcohol, marijuana, and cocaine. He has tried virtually every street drug he could get his hands on. He says the drugs have helped. Still, there's pain.

When I asked him how he received the scars on his forearms, he explained how they were self-inflicted cigarette burns and cuts. When I asked him why he merely replied, "I got really mad."

Jeremy becomes most hostile when he feels the urge to get close to someone—an urge that comes to him regularly. He punishes himself for needing people as if this will stop the need.

When he cannot medicate himself with drugs, he thinks about dying. He told me he would like to be dead but that he wouldn't feel right about committing suicide. I interpret this, perhaps foolishly, as a sign that he may still have a twinkle of hope. He doesn't seem quite ready to give up. He is almost completely without direction in life, he is in torment, and he pushes away anyone who tries to get close enough to help him. Still, he hasn't ended his struggle.

The other kids at the treatment center don't care much for Jeremy. He's always pushing people away. He has one annoying behavior that may epitomize his condition. A number of other clients like to do jigsaw puzzles in their free time. They can spend hours working to put their projects together. But since Jeremy arrived, things have changed. No one wants to work the puzzles anymore because they've learned that Jeremy has taken one piece from each puzzle. In the recreation area there are three puzzles completed except for one missing piece each. The other kids say that he has taken the pieces so that no one can finish a puzzle. He is, they say, doing it for spite.

I don't know. I can't be sure. Maybe they're right. But I think there's more to it. I think Jeremy wants someone to pursue the missing pieces. There are thousands of Jeremys in the world. Missing pieces that belong in the picture but just can't find a way to fit. They all, like Jeremy, have much to teach. Angry Jeremy, for instance, can teach us about the gruesome effects of man's inhumanity to man. His pain started early. The victim of severe child abuse as a toddler, he went on to face a series of overwhelming rejections. There's probably even more heartache and suffering inside him that he may never share. Living with the discontent of an abandoned child, Jeremy pushes away any threat of affection. If he ever tells his story, I'll bet it will move the statues.

But Jeremy is missing from the picture. He is hidden in his drugs and his anger. His tremendously important message remains unspoken.

One who is not willing to share his message may never find his own mission in life. We have a responsibility to touch the lives of others. We carry pieces of each other's calling. Part of our calling is to help others find theirs.

Addendum

Bonner was a man of few words. He spoke little and wrote even less. He didn't leave much in the way of quotations. His legacy consisted, for the most part, of stories told about his caring and generosity and, of course, his boxes of kindness. He seemed to know, intuitively, who needed a box and he made each one specially for each recipient. Some believed he was a wizard or a sorcerer or even a god. But those who knew him best knew him for what he really was, a good man. And that was his magic, his goodness.

Of the words he did leave us, there are some worth noting here. Shortly before his death, someone asked Bonner: "How should we live our lives?"

Bonner thought for a while, shook his head, shrugged his shoulders and with the voice of a humble sage said: "I don't know . . . but if you live your life as if powerful music were playing, then you may come to hear that music." Then he paused for a moment or two before completing his thought. "I think we're supposed to hear the music."

Bonner then returned to his work. Cutting, stitching, and humming.

4

HEROES AND VILLAINS

I believe it is the nature of people to be heroes,
given a chance.

James A. Autry
Love and Profit

Cruelty has its lessons. Cruel lessons. It screams them so loud that they are almost deafening. Cruelty, whether experienced directly or told in a story, stuns us and then keeps us captive for a time. It has a language unto itself. We feel its impact but it can be difficult to interpret. We each give it our own meanings. We each take our own lessons from cruelty. Some use cruelty to learn cruelty. Others survive it and reach kindness.

One of the most amazing facts of life is that there are so many good, caring people who carry deep scars of cruelty. They teach us that compassion sometimes has its roots in pain.

There is at least one truth about cruelty that we can all agree on. *It exists.* To deny the existence of evil would involve more than turning off our televisions. It would mean turning off reality. Tales of brutality flow regularly through all forms of the media. Many of us live in environments where cruelty surfaces routinely. And those who choose to wall themselves off from life in order to protect themselves from any harm may—even in their security—be those most victimized by evil.

56

I have suggested that kindness spreads like a Vine. In this chapter we will examine the extremes. We will consider examples of selfless giving as well as utter hatred. In between these extremes we will consider those who lose their kindness. In short, we will look at those who join the Vine as well as those who seek to destroy it. Beyond this, we need to try to understand those who have fallen from the Vine.

Heroes

In North Little Rock, Arkansas, when floods reached record levels and forced people from their homes, one local resident who lived on higher ground took in seventeen of her neighbors. These guests lived there for several weeks until their homes were repaired.[1] In Onekama, Michigan, the locals took out personal loans totaling eighty-five thousand dollars to enable a neighbor to rebuild his grocery store which had burned down.[2] In St. Charles, Missouri, hundreds of people turned out in the rain to assist in the search for two missing young boys. In times of crisis, perhaps more than at any other time, compassion shows its strength.

Events barely noticed by the world seem to keep it spinning. If we hope to understand what it means to be human or how the world survives, we need to consider these events. They can help maintain our faith in ourselves and the future of humankind.

Kindness can arise in the strangest places. Many of us, for instance, might not think of motorcycle gangs as particularly altruistic. Yet while researching this book, I met an area coordinator for the Special Olympics who told me that one of their local volunteer directors is the leader of a motorcycle gang. So, at least for a while, the world will keep turning—fueled by countless (and often unnoticed) acts of kindness.

Then there is Sondra. A teacher for over twenty years, and one of the very best around, she has collected a number of awards and accolades for excellence in teaching. In spite of this recognition, she doesn't feel especially proud of her performance. In truth, she would be the last person to tell you about the awards. She simply goes about her business devoting tremendous amounts of talent and energy to the education and welfare of children.

It would be a mistake to say that Sondra has a high self-esteem. At best, it's probably in the normal range. At worst, it can drop to levels that can be troublesome. You see, in Sondra's mind, all her caring and compassionate acts do not make her the least bit special. She's not in it for her ego. She is simply doing what she believes is right. One might say that the awards do not make sense to her. After all, no one gives awards to people for breathing. It's too natural to praise. So she wonders, "Why make such a fuss about it? It's just something that needs to be done."

Sondra is hardly a joyous person, but she has a vibrant child in her that makes itself apparent. Her humor is keen, though often self-disparaging. She is quite at home with children. I guess you could say that's where she belongs.

But Sondra began taking care of people long before she became a teacher. She was one of eight children. Both her parents were chronically ill. Her father suffered from a variety of physical ailments and was bedridden and hospitalized during much of Sondra's childhood. Her mother, on the other hand, had a long history of serious mental illness. Consequently, Sondra (the oldest child) assumed many of the parental responsibilities in the home. She not only cared for her siblings, but also for her parents. This was made even more difficult by her mother's bizarre behavior.

Sondra recalls that when she was eight years old, her family lived in a rural area near a railroad station. Each night, before bedtime, her mother would remove the baby from his crib and take him outside and leave him on the front porch. Mother explained that she was leaving the infant so he could be taken by "the railroad men." And each night after mother left the newborn on the porch and wandered off to bed, Sondra would retrieve the baby and return him safely to his crib. The next night the process would repeat itself. This went on for months.

Sondra pays humanity quite a compliment when she says she is nothing special. All the kindnesses she has conveyed in her life are, she says, "nothing that anyone else wouldn't have done." What's striking about her kind ways is that they are so natural. She has angry moments and sad moments and, on occasion I'm sure, selfish moments. Even so, her life seems filled with compassionate moments. She moves gracefully toward those who might be in need. She never seems to hesitate or second-guess how her kindnesses might affect her. Her ego does not appear to be part of her formula for caring.

I once asked Sondra what the rewards were for her kindness. Upon hearing my question, she looked disappointed as if to say, "Oh, I thought you understood." At the time, I did not. But now, I think I do. The need for rewards makes little sense to truly caring people. They act because they feel the need and hear the call. Not because the act produces a happy ending.

During the Vietnam War, sixty-three Medals of Honor were awarded to soldiers who threw themselves on explosive devices, in most cases hand grenades, in order to protect their comrades. Of these sixty-three men, only four lived. Sociologist Joseph A. Blake researched this phenomenon and reached an interesting, but not surprising, conclusion. He found that "the more cohesive a combat group was, the greater the likelihood that it would produce such acts; those who committed them had sacrificed themselves not for the group's military goals but for the other men in it."[3] The feeling of connectedness explains much heroism. Heroes are not really links of a chain; they are branches on a Vine. A Vine, unlike a chain, grows and is capable of connecting us in many directions. The Vine that connects has a way of providing extraordinary courage.

The Oliners's study found a strong sense of connectedness among those who risked their lives to rescue Jews during the Holocaust. Rescuers, they found, were "definitely more empathic and more easily moved by pain than nonrescuers." But what is most intriguing concerns the relationship they found between altruism and self-esteem. As I mentioned previously, Sondra—one of the kindest people I have ever known—was not someone who could be accurately described as having a high self-esteem. She frequently spoke of how those she worked with were more talented than she and how her friends were better mothers than she could ever be. She didn't envy these friends; she admired them. She didn't see herself as being "on their level," but that didn't make them any less likeable. She was good at respecting people.

At first I thought Sondra was a fluke. I had this notion that people who were as kind as she must have lots of self-esteem. I had seen the research studies that have demonstrated how children who have a high self-esteem are more likely to be generous. I guess I just concluded that the same held true for adults.

I've since learned that this is not the case. I now understand that some of the most caring people around are not completely self-confident. Sometimes this is because they tend to the needs of others exclusively. Consequently, they take too little time to care for themselves.

Another complication here is that it can be difficult to measure self-esteem. Caring people are usually quite humble. Humility can be confused with a low self-esteem. Both groups of individuals downplay their abilities. There is, however, an important distinction between the two. People who have developed a healthy humility have a contentment about them. They realize that they have limitations and they accept this. It's O.K. to be less than perfect. Folks with little self-esteem, on the other hand, rarely feel this contentment. Their imperfections are too threatening. They don't respect and admire; they resent and envy. They see their limitations but they won't accept them. Since they tend to stay focused on unacceptable parts of themselves, they may come to see only the flaws.

You're not likely to catch humble people bragging much. They see little point in it. Furthermore, they see little benefit in convincing you they have plenty of self-confidence. What does it matter? Humble people are not looking to buy a high self-esteem. They seem content to feel good enough. Although they frequently achieve great things, they do not need to feel better than anyone. They need only to feel good enough. We might call this feeling serenity.

Thus, it makes sense that the Oliners's study of Holocaust rescuers found that "rescuers had no more favorable views of themselves than did nonrescuers."[4] The Oliners explained their finding this way: "The absence of a connection between self-esteem and altruism should not be surprising. People who are sufficiently content with themselves might feel freer to attend to others' needs, but because of their high self-image might also regard themselves as appropriate recipients of attention and care from others, rather than bestowers."[5]

High self-esteem may be the twentieth century's most overrated condition. At some point, as self-esteem rises, it can turn into self-centeredness and then, ultimately, into isolation. In order to feel good about yourself all the time, you would have to cut yourself off from the rest of the world. How could rescuers feel good about being a part of humanity when they knew of fellow human beings leading children into gas chambers? And how did it feel for them to know this and, at the same time, realize that they could not stop it? All they could do, though immensely courageous and helpful, was not enough.

The rescuers were the ones who felt the greatest sense of connectedness. They felt an attachment not only to all of humankind but also to the spirit within us and beyond us that moves us toward compassion. Although people call the spirit different names, it seems to know each of our names. If we listen, it has a way of reaching us. The rescuers were not the most talented, powerful, or self-assured. But they were the ones willing and humble enough to be touched. They didn't have the most wonderful self-image, but they probably had the deepest spirit.

We live in an era where a highly positive self-esteem is seen as the foundation of all emotional health and happiness. But

I think we need to reexamine this. Will Rogers once remarked, "It's great to be great. But it's greater to be human." I think we would be a happier, healthier people if we worked more at being good human beings and less at being great.

Another important consideration here concerns courage. An important question arises. Do you have to have courage before you can be caring? This question is especially relevant when we consider acts of heroism. Those soldiers who threw themselves on grenades to protect their friends, for example. Were these the men with the most courage? Did they feel fear? Or was it a move made on impulse without emotion?

Popular author Gerald G. Jampolsky says that "when someone is occupied with helping another person, he experiences no fear."[6] Although his point is well taken, with one small alteration it becomes even more accurate. When someone is occupied with helping another person, *he finds courage*. Courage is not the absence of fear; it is the force that carries us through fear. Caring and compassion provide us with a purpose. Courage gives us the means to achieve that purpose. Furthermore, compassion has a way of leading us to the source of courage. We feel this source while in the act of caring. It can carry us through overwhelming fear.

You do not have to be courageous before you can become compassionate. Acts of caring generate their own courage. Again, if you allow yourself to be moved, you will be moved. As you move you find courage. Even while moving through fear.

Compassionate people may be our best examples of courage. They teach simple yet profound lessons. Tragedies teach cruel lessons. Heroes teach hope. We live on a planet where cruelty and kindness coexist. At times, we all face the decision whether we want to be bystanders or heroes. (Hero, of course, is another word for a good human being.)

In order to be a hero we do not have to begin with vast amounts of courage or a flawless self-image. Instead, we need only feel the connectedness that joins humanity. If we touch the feeling, then we will be moved with great courage to care for the people and things that matter to us. And these people and things will be many.

Compassion Fatigue

I called the American Red Cross recently to ask if there was a limit to how much blood a person could donate. I wanted to know at what point the Red Cross would refuse to accept any more of someone's blood.

I found out that under normal circumstances, you can give one "unit" (i.e., slightly less than one pint) at a time and that the Red Cross will not allow you to make another donation until fifty-six days later. The spokesperson told me that this policy was designed to protect "the health and welfare of our donors."

It's a simple truth. You can give only so much blood before you begin to hurt yourself. No matter how well intended you may be, you can give only so much blood. If you give all your blood at once, you'll bleed to death. Then there will be no more to give. There will be nothing to replenish.

If, however, you donate one unit at a time and then wait the proper interval before making your next donation, you will be able to make countless contributions. Over the long run, your gifts will be much more numerous than had you emptied yourself in a single dying effort. You will be building yourself to become a person capable of making ongoing and lasting contributions. In order to maximize what you can give, you have to protect your ability to give. If not, you may give out.

Nature provides all its creatures with some form of protection. Roses have thorns. Clams have shells. Deer have speed. Skunks have their odor. There's certainly nothing wrong with protection. Even churches have locks. But we are unique in that we need more than just protection from *external* threats. We need knowledge and attitudes that will help protect us from ourselves. Even with all the best intentions, we are quite capable of self-destruction. In fact, it might not be too far-fetched to suggest that the most common form of destructiveness today could be self-destruction.

We have only so much blood to give. No matter how desperate the need, we have only so much blood. If we try to give more than we have, we run out completely.

Psychologically, when you run out of blood you fall into compassion fatigue. Author and syndicated columnist Dolores Curran writes: "Simply defined, compassion fatigue means we get weary of feeding the hungry, hearing about the homeless, and caring about those in the Third World." Once it sets in, caring becomes a foolish burden. It no longer makes sense to attempt to help anyone. It's the feeling of having cared and failed.

Compassion fatigue rarely seizes a person all at once. Typically, it moves in like a slow infection, silently spreading until it gains control of its victims. Once exhausted, the victim may feel trapped and filled with resentment, depression, and guilt. The victim may develop a cynical nature. Loving acts that he or she at one time considered quite moving are now looked on with disdain as stupid and naive. The warm-hearted soul has now become bitter. It is as if one's spirit has been removed from one's system.

Here lies one of the most important points about compassion fatigue. *It afflicts only those who were once compassionate.* This is how we are losing many of the truly caring souls in our midst. Compassion fatigue explains how young idealists become discontented misers and how bold dreamers turn into selfish hoarders. Our planet cannot afford to lose a single caring idealist or dearmer, yet I'm afraid it happens all too often. Compassion fatigue is a devastating condition.

We don't need an in-depth analysis of how the problem develops. Kindness can be an effort and, like all efforts, sometimes the desired ends are not reached. Repeated frustration can drain even the strongest and most resolute hero. Kind people tend to be sensitive. They can be hurt. A suit of armor can impede their mission so it is usually discarded. They go into the fray undisguised and often inadequately protected. Frequently they become wounded so deeply that they leave their will to help on the field of need . . . and then refuse to retrieve it.

Many times compassion fatigue is rooted in fear. Fear of what might happen should the victim decide to try again. Keep in mind that these victims are people who were once generous, caring beings. Love and compassion are integral parts of their characters. No exhaustion, no matter how severe, can erase this. Compassion fatigue keeps its victims from being true to themselves. It puts a coating of ice around a warm heart. The heart may shrink but it never disappears. Compassion fatigue may keep people from acting on their feelings, but it does not kill the feelings. The behavior may change, and so too may one's spoken beliefs, but the feelings don't. The desire to help lives on inside a hurt, scared, tired, and sometimes bitter soul.

When people decide that "It's no use anymore" they may grasp certain worn philosophies to rationalize their conversion. A lot of times these philosophies focus on the nature of the Real World. Statements such as "I used to think it was my responsibility to love my neighbor but now I know that that's not how things work in the Real World," and "In the Real World you have to protect what's yours" point to the belief that we live in a place where it's not safe to care. In this place only the foolish and those too dimwitted to see what's real dare offer a hand to help.

This mythical land called the Real World appears to be a really ugly place. People caught in this nightmare act as if they are glad they can finally see things for what they are. In the Real World you shouldn't get your feelings hurt because you're not supposed to let them show. That would be idiotic. But no one is happy either. Such a pathetic place.

Compassion fatigue leads its victims to the Real World. It feels like a refuge at first but it soon becomes a trap. A trap whose power lies in the fact that its victims are too drained and tired to fight it. Furthermore, they may not even see it for what it is. For a while, a trap can seem like security.

Perhaps every caring individual runs into bouts of compassion fatigue. Dolores Curran suggests that even Jesus may have had encounters with it. "He must have become weary of so many people asking to be healed. But we also know that he went out into the desert occasionally to get away and pray, to refresh his spirit so that he could return and minister to others."

We may be able to prevent a good deal of kindness burnout by simply being aware of our susceptibility to it. But if it hits us, it can help to have a strategy for getting out of it. There's a certain amount of wear and tear that comes with being a good person. We need to know how to repair ourselves.

In an effort to assist those in need of repair, I am proposing an eight-step strategy for restoring a lost spirit. Should you ever find yourself at a point where you feel incapable of offering the caring and kindness you once could, consider the following procedure. It is intended to help rescue you from the Real World.

1. *Become aware of the problem.* One trouble with compassion fatigue is that it can disguise itself as an awakening of sorts. The afflicted often express new attitudes such as, "It took me long enough to get it through my thick skull, but I've finally realized that it's best to look out for numero uno!" The immediate impact of this change can seem like a relief, sometimes a big relief. Deciding not to be concerned about the problems of others can feel quite freeing for a time. After all, kindness can be a burden.

After what can be a short-term euphoria, the discontent starts to take root. It moves so quietly that it can go unnoticed. The victim gradually realizes that something is wrong but may be completely unaware of what it is.

Understanding that one has become burned out on giving and sharing is the first step toward recovery. Knowing where we are helps reduce the confusion and begins to point us in the direction of a remedy. Among other things, this awareness can teach us that we may need to take better care of ourselves.

Actually, this is what compassion fatigue is all about—taking care of ourselves. Although this is often misinterpreted as selfishness, this is not the proper description. If we can identify our compassion fatigue, we will understand that what we are feeling is not selfishness but rather the need for self-care. Feeling selfish leads to cynicism and more selfishness. Feeling the need to care for oneself leads to recovery and rebirth.

2. *Decide to do something about the problem.* This condition begins to improve as soon as you give your permission to do something about it. While certain strategies are more effective than others, the fact that you are willing to act is in itself healing. If you have a history of devoting yourself to the needs of others, you may have forgotten *how* to care for yourself. Even worse, you may have never learned.

When all is said and done, trial and error may be our most natural form of learning. We need to keep in mind that "error" means "learning" rather than "failure." If we make a conscious effort to nourish and sustain ourselves physically, emotionally, intellectually, and spiritually then, at the very least, we will be learning how to vitalize ourselves. It's a win/win proposition. The effort is what counts here. You begin taking care of yourself when you start looking for ways to treat yourself. You start to come alive as soon as you prepare yourself to act.

When we change our thinking from "What's wrong with me?" to "What can I do about my situation?" we move much closer to action. This new mindset actually starts us moving.

3. *Be kind to yourself.* It's amazing how many people are afraid to be good to themselves. Some folks, I guess, confuse this with self-centeredness or conceit. Others may be concerned that they will be seen as vain or shallow. Still others probably fear being envied. While it can be difficult distinguishing legitimate reasons from excuses, the fact remains that being good to ourselves can, for some, be much more challenging than it sounds.

If we don't take care of ourselves, we will not be of much help to others. Exhaustion sets in on those unwilling or incapable of replenishing themselves. The bottom line is that if you are not good to yourself, you may lose your capacity to care for others.

Being kind to yourself can take more forms than there are people on earth. You can take a vacation or just stay home and take a nap. You can write your memoirs or sit in an easy chair and read the comics. You can go to a nostalgic high-school reunion or sit in solitude to pray or meditate. No matter what you do, look for things you love. Look for things you call your *favorites*. Your favorite friends, foods, movies, books, music, places, memories, games, challenges, teams, sports, speakers, clothes, art, and hobbies. You can have as many favorites as you want. Happy people know that "favorite" does *not* mean "just one." For instance, you can have as many favorite memories as you want.

The only favorites you need to lose are your favorite excuses for not taking care of yourself. If you have avoided treating yourself, you may feel foolish once you start, foolish because you waited so long. Then there's the fear. But all this really amounts to is a fear that you might like it. Being good to yourself can lead to real personal growth which, though healthy, can be frightening. Getting healthy can be scary.

Being kind to yourself is an essential component of compassion. It keeps you from running out of things to give.

4. *Find your birds of a feather.* You're not alone. Compassion fatigue is more common than you may think. If you are in the midst of this condition, have the courage to talk about it. Find a good listener (or a few good listeners) and pour your heart out. If that person listens carefully and sincerely wants to help, then the two probably have a lot in common. She may even have experienced bouts of compassion fatigue herself.

Support helps revive your ethic of caring. Unfortunately, chronic caretakers can have a tough time asking for help for themselves. So this step isn't always as easy as it sounds. Sometimes the only experience that can convince one to ask for help is more suffering. Indeed this is one of suffering's most powerful lessons—people need people. Some people never learn it and they melt away tormented and alone.

Once you have found or created support for yourself you will feel your energy build. You may tap an impulse that drives you to get right back on the horse. This is not wise, not yet anyway. Give yourself time to heal. Let your support help you.

5. *Reevaluate your stamina and your pace.* Look at the events that produced your burnout. Were you making sound choices? Were you giving too much blood at a time? We all have limitations. If we don't accept this or if we don't know what our limitations are, we can drive ourselves into the ground. While we are healing, we need to consider the nature of our limitations. Then we must learn to respect them and live with them.

More than anything, this step involves acquiring a little humility. Maybe you can't be Joan of Arc or Albert Schweitzer or Mother Teresa. But you don't have to be a saint in order for your goodness to count. Do what only you can do.

6. *Observe kindness.* Kindess can make you vulnerable. When you reach out, you lower your defenses. You become even more vulnerable if you are unsure if being kind is the right thing to do. If you have come this far in your recovery from compassion fatigue, you have probably already gotten through the cynicism, but you may not have solved the uncertainty. This is the feeling: "I really would like to be a caring person, but . . ." You may not be sure what comes after the "but", but there seems to be something.

At this point you need to see compassion in action. Window shop. See if it looks right. You can find it in many places. *But you have to look for it.* You can see it in parks, playgrounds, restaurants, nursing homes, supermarkets, libraries, post offices, and shelters for the homeless. You can see it on television, hear about it on the radio and read about it in the newspapers. But remember, you have to believe it to see it.

If, in spite of your efforts, you cannot find scenes of real caring, then I suggest you return to the place where you learned to appreciate kindness. Sometimes returning to the place where something important was born can kindle a rebirth. If that birthplace no longer exists, try to get as close to it as you can, close enough to empower your memories of this special place and point in time. Then, once you can feel the memories, return to the present and see if you can find the compassion.

There are lessons and remedies in other people's kindnesses. If what you see seems right, you may lose your uncertainty.

7. *Learn from experience.* Never forget a bad experience; there's always much to learn. If you've come this far in your recovery, you've already learned a lot. But before you move on, stop to consider what you have been through. What have you learned? What have you not yet learned? Is the life of a good person worth the costs? Now that you have felt the costs, you are in a much better position to answer this.

Understand that compassion fatigue is not like the mumps; it can come again. Should you decide to reenter the arena of caring, you will not be immune to exhaustion. Let your fatigue teach you about limitations. Only when you understand your limitations will you be capable of recognizing your real power. Compassion fatigue sets in as you try to give things that you don't have to give.

Learn your limits. Find your gifts.

8. *Consciously decide whether or not and, if so, how you will exercise your compassion.* Make a choice. Don't let yourself be led back into pastures where you don't belong just because others tell you to or plead with you. This has to be your call, a decision you understand and are willing to stand behind. No one else can take responsibility for this choice.

You possess the gift of compassion. This gift, like all gifts, must be put to use. An unused gift will cause chronic emotional and spiritual turmoil. It will not go away. It is there to be actualized. If you decide to share your gift, you then need to choose the path that provides you with the energy and enthusiasm to keep the gift vibrant and life-giving. Choose carefully.

The return to caring may require a tremendous amount of courage, or it may seem like the most natural move you have ever made. It may take a few days or it can take months. You are entitled to your time to heal.

If you have the gift of kindness, you are called to use it. Those who develop compassion fatigue are among those with this gift. It afflicts only those who have the gift of caring. But then a question arises. Is there anyone without this gift?

Cruelty and Indifference

While I was growing up on the Jersey shore, our family had a housekeeper named Myrtle. Myrtle came to us before I could talk and then stayed until I was a teenager. She was black and she was born sometime around the turn of the century. She spent her childhood years living in the South. While there, she collected some of the most moving stories I've ever heard.

At first glance, Myrtle might have seemed unremarkable. She went about her work quietly, rarely bringing attention to herself. If you spent enough time with her, though, certain qualities gradually became striking. For example, if you watched closely enough, you could see that Myrtle had amazing hands. While cooking, she rarely used potholders; she would usually move the hot trays and pans with her bare hands. When I asked how she did this, she simply said: "When you touch a lot of heat, after a while your skin becomes strong." End of explanation.

Myrtle was also one of the kindest people I've ever known. A simple, loving woman, she was born strong and gentle. She had the type of kindness that you recognize slowly. Like the person you've known for some time and then one day it suddenly hits you like a bolt of lightning: "What a fine person she is!" And then you wonder how you didn't see it long ago.

One summer day around the time I turned eight, Myrtle decided it was time that I learned a little more about life. On this particular afternoon, I sat in the kitchen with her as she prepared dinner. I can't remember exactly what started the conversation, but for the first time she began telling me about the men in hoods and white robes who would come suddenly in the dead of night and take the "colored people" from their homes. The men had whips and torches. They burnt houses and barns. They beat parents while their children looked on. While they inflicted this cruelty, the men in white robes laughed and even sang.

As Myrtle continued, I sat there frozen. These tales were like nothing I had ever heard. They would have been completely unbelievable except for the fact that it was Myrtle telling them. They were stories of *her* childhood.

She told me about one particular night when the men came. They took a black minister and, in front of his congregation, covered him with tar. They tied him to the back of a car or wagon and dragged him out of town. As she spoke, I knew that she could still see these memories.

Over the next few years, I heard several more of these stories (usually because I would ask to hear them). But Myrtle never told them just to be a storyteller. She told me her stories because they needed to be told. This history has to be passed down. The human capacity for cruelty must be acknowledged. Like the men in white hoods, cruelty likes to operate in darkness and secrecy. More than anything, I think Myrtle wanted me to know that there was more to the world than was apparent in my idyllic seashore childhood. Beyond this, I believe she accomplished something else. Myrtle taught me to stop taking kindness for granted.

It serves no one to deny the existence of cruelty. It's there. Whether or not it is inevitable, I don't know. For now, it's part of our world.

We know so little about cruelty. It seems to be the nature of evil to keep anyone from getting close enough to understand it. At best, it pushes you away. It can even destroy those who come near it.

Ultimately, evil destroys the vessels that carry it. Erich Fromm, for instance, pointed out that many of the SS men who performed mass murder during the Holocaust "became sick after carrying out their mass executions; some committed suicide, became psychotic, or suffered other severe mental damage."[7] There is an element of self-destruction in every act of cruelty. We lose something of ourselves each time we seek to injure another until, finally, we've lost everything but the hatred. Those who stay in their white robes can become their white robes. They lose their humanity to hatred.

Cruelty is rooted in hurt. Evil has a way of entering the despairing, the rejected, and the abandoned. It knows that these are fertile grounds to plant hatred. Once hatred takes hold, it can be all but impossible for the afflicted to reconnect with the rest of humankind. Hatred will not allow it.

While searching for the cure to cruelty, we need to keep in mind that no one wants to carry hatred. It is not a natural state nor is it a pleasant one. Remember, hatred destroys all who carry it. People choose to carry hatred only when they believe that their only alternative is complete and utter powerlessness. We need to feel our impact on the world. If one believes that he has absolutely nothing to offer, nothing constructive to contribute, then hatred and destructiveness begin to grow. The feeling of not being able to contribute is the greatest frustration a human being can ever know. It leads to hostility, resentment, envy, outrage, and hatred. This individual feels a deep sense of betrayal. As strange as this may sound, it is as if he had been promised when he began his life that he would be living in a world where he could make real contributions. Then, if it appears to this person that he has nothing to give, he will react as if a sacred promise has been broken and that, consequently, no one can ever be trusted again. Unless this trust is reignited, the hatred remains.

Hatred is contagious. If we see enough of it, we can begin to wonder if it's human nature. This is a dangerous myth. Our behaviors tend to follow our beliefs. When we think of ourselves as a selfish or ruthless race of people, then the likelihood of building trust or sacrificing for the welfare of others dwindles.

In 1968 researcher Harvey A. Hornstein and his colleagues conducted an experiment designed to test for altruism in the big city. For several months during that year the researchers "lost" an average of forty wallets a day in New York. These wallets contained "small sums of money and sundry documents." The purpose of the study was to determine how many people would go out of their way to see that the wallets were returned to their owners. When all the results were in and they examined their data, some interesting findings emerged. How many wallets were returned? According to Hornstein, "On the average, about 45 percent of the people who found these wallets returned them." You will have to decide for yourself whether you consider this good news or bad.

This study, quite unintentionally, found something else. Over the months, the return rate stayed consistent at 45 percent. For better or worse, this was their finding. The researchers, however, noted that "during all the months that we worked, only one major exception to the general pattern occurred: not a single one of the wallets lost on June 4, 1968, was returned. During the night a bullet fired by Sirhan Sirhan smashed through the skull of Robert F. Kennedy, killing him, and simultaneously eliminating whatever motives caused people to return our fictitious stranger's lost wallet."[8]

I guess the world didn't feel very kind that day. A single act of violence made the planet grow cold. (I wonder what is lost in a single day without kindness.) A couple of days later people were returning wallets at the average rate.

I don't believe that cruelty can conquer a kind heart. With kindness comes courage and conviction that will not allow it to be permanently put to rest. Cruelty and hatred are, however, persuasive to the undecided. Evil can convince the unsettled that one's first priority should be self-protection. Once this conclusion has been reached, selfishness can seem like a moral obligation. You would do what you needed to fit in or get by. Caring might no longer be a serious option.

I also don't believe that the other 55 percent (i.e., those who did not return lost wallets) were necessarily bad or dishonest. If we could have studied this group, I think we would have found that many of these people were part of the clan called *the indifferents*. Folks in this group frequently inflate themselves by saying things like, "I wouldn't hurt a fly." The trouble is, they wouldn't go out of their way to help one either.

The old western movies had a knack for depicting the indifferents. The high-noon showdown between the hero and the villain symbolized the struggle between good and evil. If you notice, there's always a large group of bystanders lining the street to watch the face-off. Most of these people wouldn't hurt a fly. But they are willing to let the good guy stand alone and risk his life. Fortunately, in all the westerns I've ever seen, the hero won the duel. Lucky for him that he did because if he didn't, I'm not sure the indifferents would have handed him even a bandage.

It seems that whenever there is misfortune, there are bystanders. People so afraid or so indifferent that they appear immovable. People have found a million and one reasons to sit and watch life go by. But even with a front-row seat, the parade is not always a happy one. As it passes, one can see sorrow, hurt, loneliness, fear, poverty, disease, starvation, and despair. If you choose to be a spectator, you can insulate yourself only for so long. If you try to turn away from the parade, you will find that it surrounds you.

Indifference and cowardice become bitterness. Then the big moment arrives when you hear your own voice speaking within you saying, "I wish I would have given more." As the impact of this statement rattles through you, you will find yourself desperately hoping that it is not too late to start.

We can resist the call to compassion, but this resistance will never make us happy. Many people can point to a long list of hurts in their lives and use these lists to support the opinion that you should care only for yourself. And though logic might say they're right, I've never known a person with such an attitude to find contentment. A recent article in a popular magazine discusses a woman who keeps a "hate book." "Every time her husband of twelve years does something to annoy or

offend her, she writes it down in her book and says to herself,
'another nail in your coffin.'"⁹ If you look for nails, you will
find them. If you hoard them, you will be over your head in
nails. Bitter people can usually explain very well why they are
bitter. They can show you the nails they've collected. Ultimately, however, they are nails in their own coffins. Bitterness
eventually takes the life right out of you.

Alcoholics Anonymous has for decades been warning its
members about the damage caused by carrying resentments.
This advice applies equally well to everyone. In order to find
health, we must deal with and then let go of our resentments or
they will tear us apart. AA encourages its members to develop a
different kind of list, a gratitude list. A gratitude list keeps you
in touch with all you have to be thankful for. Later we will
give more attention to the power of gratitude, but for now it
is important to understand that gratitude helps keep us from
drowning in resentments. Gratitude and resentment are not
compatible. Your psyche and soul are not big enough for the
both of them.

But what are the costs to those who cling to their hatreds?
What is the extent of the damage? Rabbi Harold Kushner once
pointed out that "Ultimately, the selfish, mean, nasty person
will be punished, even if his only punishment is that he will
never know the satisfaction of being a good person."¹⁰ This is
a consequence we often overlook—never knowing the satisfaction of being a good person. This satisfaction may be one of
the greatest rewards life has to offer. Missing it may be one of
life's biggest tragedies.

In the next chapter we will deal in more detail with resentments. We will consider forgiveness as a road to removing
hatred from one's heart. Before we end this section, we must
emphasize the fact that becoming a good person can be a struggle. Even though a good person does not have to be, nor can
ever be, a perfect person, it can be hard enough just being
good. Being a caring, concerned human being means making
a statement with your behavior. There will be others who may

not appreciate your sacrifices because your sacrifices will place an expectation on them to do the same. Not everyone is ready to make sacrifices.

Poet Maya Angelou warned that, "We've come to a time when one has to apologize for saying that I want to be a good human being." It's not easy being a hero. It's not easy being a good human being. But then the two are really the same. Our heroes are no longer shooting it out with the bad guys at high noon. Our heroes are handing out bandages, donating blood, volunteering time and energy, giving encouragement, and lending a hand. Each of these acts adds an item to someone's gratitude list. And thus the Vine grows.

I guess that being a good person means apologizing to the bystanders and then courageously walking out into the light of the noonday sun to face your fears in order to build a better universe. Even when the indifferents call you back, you keep walking. As you walk, you feel the courage build. You see the mean and nasty, but you refuse to let them run your life. As you walk, even though it may appear at times that you are completely unnoticed, you become a hero.

5

FORGIVENESS

Without forgiveness, life is governed by an
endless cycle of resentment and retaliation.
Roberto Assagioli

When I first outlined this book, it had only seven chapters, the *other* seven chapters. The final major addition
reflects what may be the most important lesson I've learned
while writing this. As I learned more and more, it became
clear that a book on kindness would not be complete without
a chapter on forgiveness.

I came to this conclusion while looking for answers to the
question, "How does one become free of bitterness?" The answer seems simple once it's found. So simple that it leads one
to wonder how it could ever be missed.

Martin Luther King, Jr. claimed that "we must develop and
maintain the capacity to forgive. He who is devoid of the power
to forgive is devoid of the power to love." Love and forgiveness
sustain each other. It's not easy being a loving person in an
imperfect world. Sometimes the love isn't returned. Sometimes
the love is taken away. Those who live loving and caring lives
are those who can return to their kind ways even after they
are reminded that love can lead to hurt.

Losing the ability to forgive means losing the ability to love.
For those who have lost their forgiveness, finding it again
means becoming reacquainted with their spirit. In his fine book

Teach Only Love, Gerald G. Jampolsky writes, "Forgiveness is the means whereby we experience peace, know ourselves as love, give without sacrifice, join the essence of others, experience fully this instant, and hear clearly the inner counselings of happiness." When the spirit reemerges, it can perform miracles on the mind and the body.

On the other side of the coin, carrying bitterness and resentment can wreak havoc on the human system. The late, eminent stress researcher Hans Selye taught that feelings of revenge and hate are injurious to our physical health. They tighten the back, ache the head, or eat through the stomach. Bitterness doesn't stay put. It keeps attacking. We can release it, but we cannot (if we hold on to it) control it. Those who live with hatred live with a tyrant. People who hate come to hate themselves. We cannot control hate well enough to keep it pointed outward. Eventually it will assault everything it can, including the person who carries it. Holding on to bitterness, resentment, and hatred is like holding on to fire. While they burn, they destroy. As long as we keep them inside us, they have a will of their own.

Hatred clouds the psyche and drains the spirit. It robs us of the ability to think clearly and hinders our capacity to rationally examine the causes and consequences of our anger. A confused mind is easier to manipulate. In the throes of this confusion, individuals can develop beliefs to justify their rage.

Once the venom of hatred has impacted the mind, the spirit can also be wounded. Because the spirit is a necessary force in the forgiveness process, its absence can leave one a slave to one's hostility. Conversely, empowering the spirit is essential to recovery. Even when our brain tells us we have every right to stay resentful, the spirit (if we give it the power by giving it our attention) has a way of reminding us that this resentment is only useless baggage that weighs us down and keeps us from being moved. Our spirit seeks to live in harmony with all forms of life.

Maybe theologian Lewis B. Smedes was right when he wrote, "Forgiveness is God's invention for coming to terms with a world in which, despite their best intentions, people are unfair to each other and hurt each other deeply. He began by forgiving us. And He invites us all to forgive each other."[1] Thriving in an imperfect world requires forgiveness. Those who seek to explore, learn, and love must be *prepared* to forgive. In a full life, there will be disappointments. People who can continue to move and marvel in spite of the hurts are the people who will know real contentment. They refuse to absorb the expectation that life is a journey without pain. They know they will have to grow beyond the hurts. Contented souls eventually forgive, let go, and then move on. You must face your life ready to forgive.

"When you forgive someone for hurting you," continued Smedes, "you perform spiritual surgery inside your soul; you cut away the wrong that was done to you so that you can see your 'enemy' through the magic eyes that can heal your soul."[2] This "spiritual surgery" is so important. People with deep wounds sometimes try to pretend their injuries have healed. These people genuinely want to be good-hearted. They even fantasize about themselves being generous and loving. But they can't get through the bitterness that started with past hurts. Because their resentment keeps them from becoming the people they would like to be, they fall far short of their ideal image of themselves. If they are unable to work through the bitterness, they will slowly become deeply ashamed of themselves. Once shame takes root, a person can stop trying to give or contribute. The essence of shame is the conviction that one has nothing to offer. Without anything of value to provide, one feels anything but kind.

Traveling the road back to spiritual health means releasing the bitterness. With this breakthrough comes the feeling that your spirit once again is a part of you. Forgiveness is the process of reclaiming your spirit. With this reclamation comes a renewed energy and direction. The spirit connects people with people.

Forgiveness is a necessary dimension of kindness. Compassionate people have a knack for working themselves free of grudges. Will Rogers once advised, "Don't let yesterday use up too much of today." Kind people realize the importance of today and refuse to get caught up in issues that would detract from what they can do in the present. When they run into the hurts that are part of life, they deal with them to the best of their ability and then go on. Each time they forgive, they become a little better at it.

Eventually, it becomes a way of life.

Understanding

When Alexander Chase wrote, "To understand is to forgive, even oneself," he summarized much of what has been learned about forgiveness through the ages. Forgiveness requires at least a bit of understanding, sometimes quite a bit. The most direct way to acquire an understanding is through an apology. An apology usually includes an explanation for why the offender acted the way he did. Once we understand why we were hurt, we find it much easier to let go of the anger and hurt. In fact, it's not at all uncommon for two people to become closer than they ever were after a sincere apology.

What's important to know about an apology is that it is more of a process than a single act. More often than not, an apology is a way of saying, "Let's enter into a relationship where we can work to heal old wounds." Simply saying "I'm sorry" only remedies the smallest stings. It will not mend a trust that has been betrayed. Trust must be rebuilt and this only *begins* with an apology. The behavior that follows proves the sincerity of the apology and gives it power. Saying "I'm sorry" can open the way for healing to begin. If it is accompanied by honesty and vulnerability and followed by the type of behavioral change that would indicate a real desire to improve the relationship, then there is hope that even devastating heartache can be overcome.

Apologies help us understand why we were hurt. This by itself can be therapeutic. Knowing why makes life more comprehensible and thus safer. If we understand how and why we were hurt, we become better prepared to avoid anguish in the future. But perhaps most importantly, when we start to understand the actions of someone who has hurt us, we also begin to empathize with that person. Just as empathy leads to compassion, it also opens the door to forgiveness. Understanding someone is a part of empathy. It is almost impossible to resent someone with whom you empathize. Empathy warms the bitterness and the hurt.

We could go on forever paying tribute to the apology. Think of what life would be like if no one had ever discovered this process of mending broken people and relationships. Few events incite as much personal growth as an apology. An honest apology can be worth more than a thousand hours of marriage counseling.

There are good apologies and bad apologies. Insincere apologies have a way of making matters worse. Honest, heartfelt apologies can make the world right again. And then there are times when there are no apologies. You probably won't hear an apology for every hurt you receive. Sometimes, perhaps frequently, you will have to work through the process of forgiving all by yourself.

Even when you are left to forgive someone who doesn't care enough to ask for your forgiveness, understanding still plays a crucial role. When the person who has hurt you will not or cannot explain his actions, it can help to have someone else willing to understand what you've been through. Being heard, or what is sometimes referred to as "telling your story," has a way of nurturing forgiveness. It helps to have another human being recognize and acknowledge your pain. Feeling the empathy speeds the healing. Sharing hurt is often the first step in letting it go.

As an example, consider the story of Janet. I first met her when she was twenty years old. Janet came to my office saying she needed counseling because she felt as if she was "living in a box that keeps getting smaller and smaller." It wasn't long before Janet began telling me her story. She had been raised by a sadistic father who claimed at times to be John the Baptist and that it was his right and duty to abuse her physically, sexually, and emotionally. He did all this, he said, for her own good. It served to "cleanse her," he insisted. He continued to abuse her throughout her childhood and adolescence.

When I asked Janet where her mother was while all this went on, she replied: "All she would do was keep apologizing for what my father did." Then, after a moment of silence and with downcast eyes, she added: "But she never did anything to stop it."

Like other abused children, Janet came to believe that she deserved this torment, that she had somehow brought it on herself. Furthermore, it appeared that she was holding on to the possibility that her father was actually a special servant of God. After all, her father appeared to be more powerful than any human laws. He did whatever he wanted without observable guilt or consequence.

Janet's stories were enough to move a stone. She was routinely threatened with damnation if she did not submit to her father. She was beaten and kept in darkened closets whenever her father deemed it appropriate. The name-calling and criticism were constant. For Janet, it must have felt like her box would never open.

Shortly after I began working with her, however, we were able to arrange for her to be moved into a shelter for abused women. Although it was a difficult adjustment at first, she came to appreciate living in a safe environment. As she began to feel the power and comfort of this safety, she opened up more and more. Between her work with me and her treatment at the shelter, Janet learned the value of telling her story.

Listening to Janet's litany of abuses was an exercise in self-control. It's terribly frustrating to hear such accounts. It's the feeling of being moved but having nothing to do or nowhere to go. You want to remove the pain by erasing the horrible experiences altogether. As I reminded myself for the millionth time that we cannot change the past, I began to reach a deeper understanding of Janet. She couldn't change the past either. She could, however, release much of the pain and free herself to create positive, healthy experiences in the future.

Ideally, Janet's father would have helped in this process. He did not. He made it clear that he wanted nothing more to do with her. She felt disposable, used, and then thrown away. There was little hope that her father would ever help her understand what she had been through. There would be no apologies.

Still, Janet would need to find a way to forgive. In order to build a future, she would have to free herself from her past and invest her attention and energies into creating a healthy life. She would have to forgive her father without his help. She would have to forgive without ever really understanding why her father did the things he did.

Janet gradually realized that she could learn to forgive even without her father's permission and apology. She learned to take a secondary path to forgiveness. One begins this particular path by allowing someone else to understand one's hurt. Janet was not allowed to be close enough to empathize with her father. Consequently, she could not reach forgiveness through this route. So she began her journey toward forgiveness by allowing others to empathize with her. She courageously told her story in grisly detail. She brought it to the surface for the purpose of, ultimately, letting it go. As she grew to feel understood, her sense of isolation lessened. As time passed, she began to reach out and help new residents of the shelter. As she lightened her load, she found she had room to carry some of someone else's.

Janet was an adult before she met acceptance. She had no money. The shelter housed her free of charge until they arranged a job for her and then they charged her only a minimal amount. For our sessions together, Janet paid in artwork. A gifted artist, her drawings served as powerful illustrations of her story. Even if she had the money, I don't think I could have charged her. In working with Janet, I felt as if somehow I was working to pay off a debt I owed, as if I were part of the world that hurt her.

She had trouble comprehending why people were being "so nice" to her. She certainly had little experience receiving kindness. Understandably, she approached it cautiously. Miraculously, this soul, who had plenty of reasons to be filled with hate, grew truly compassionate.

Of all the lessons I learned from Janet, one insight deserves special mention here. It has to do with how different hurts affect different people.

As Janet began to open up, she found that the "box" that entrapped her began to open as well. Like Pandora's box, Janet's was filled with some awful things. But unlike Pandora's story, Janet's box was filled with things that needed to get out. Their release was not a mistake. Instead it was a major step in a healing process.

Janet told of some of the most horrible experiences I have ever heard. Yet as terrible as these accounts were, I had the sense that she was holding on to something more hurtful than anything she had told me. My intuition said her worst story had yet to be told. My head, however, insisted: "How could there be anything worse?"

The months passed. Janet had some bad times. On several occasions she felt suicidal but never acted on these impulses. For a short time, without the knowledge of the staff at the shelter, she worked as a prostitute. Janet struggled with the fact that her family never tried to contact her. In spite of all that had happened, she had held on to the hope that one day they would be a happy, healthy family. As these dreams faded, so did much of her hope.

Janet, however, possessed a remarkable gift for survival. She was not yet ready to give up. But before she could really reinvest herself in life, she needed to tell one more story.

I waited as long as I could. After making a major improvement in her life by leaving home, she was now stuck in a limbo of sorts and was beginning to fear that the future would be just as painful as the past. I felt she was holding on to a story that needed to be told. That in one way or another this mysterious experience was keeping her from moving on.

After several months of counseling, I finally said to her, "You know, Janet, I have this feeling that in spite of all you've told me, there's something pretty important that you're holding on to. For a while that was O.K., but I think it's time to share it."

I didn't have to say another word. She knew what I meant. She lowered her head, stared at the floor, and in a voice just above a whisper she asked, "Have you ever been spit on?"

I paused for a moment and then quietly answered, "No . . . no I haven't." Then after another moment or two of silence I added, "Have you?"

Without lifting her head she nodded. Her focus remained on the floor, and yet it appeared as if inside her head she was reliving what psychologists call "a major life event." Never before had I seen her so tuned into a single thought. It was as if she were about to unleash a monster that had been ruling her life.

"I was seventeen," she said slowly. "I was a senior in high school. I was walking by the place where they park the school buses. I didn't do anything to him but some boy stuck his head out one of the school-bus windows and spit in my hair. I began to cry and everyone laughed. They just laughed . . . just laughed."

Her distress was obvious. My first impulse was to rescue her. I wanted to tell her that as humiliating as this must have been, it paled in comparison with the other abuses she had known. She had been tormented and neglected for as long as she could remember. How was it that this event was so much worse than the rest?

Before I spoke a word, however, I recalled the words of an old mentor, one of the best counselors I have ever known, who insisted that while treating a client, "If you don't know what to say—shut up!" So shut up I did, and slowly Janet explained in her own way why the spitting incident was so devastating.

Janet had an extraordinary imagination. Her imagination helped protect her from the insults and injuries that had bombarded her. Specifically, Janet always saw happy endings. Even when life at home was at its worst, in her mind she saw herself winning the Miss America Pageant or becoming a movie star or a great singer or famous artist. Somehow, someway, she was always going to "show them." Given her circumstances, some might call this insanity, but I prefer to view it as evidence of the amazing resiliency that comes with being human.

Her hope and imagination survived years of cruelty. They carried her to the verge of adulthood. Then came a change. Although not unattractive, she was not a candidate for a beauty contest. No one had ever asked her to audition for the school play. She liked music but finally had to admit she couldn't sing well. And even though she had been told that her artwork had potential, no one ever indicated that it could make her dreams come true. She felt she was getting close to the *someday* she had dreamed about, but it didn't look anything like the way her imagination pictured it. Then, as all this turned in her head, she started walking home from school. A few minutes later she would be spit upon and, for the first time, defeated. No more dreams.

As Janet filled in the pieces of this story, I realized what she had just taught me. This single humiliation (which seemed small in comparison to her other wounds) was to her the straw that broke the camel's back. I learned then and there to let people decide for themselves what hurts. If we decide for them, we will never understand them. And if they never come to feel understood, they may never forgive and heal.

Janet, by the way, never really needed fame or fortune. She, like everyone else, needed to be loved, respected, and appreciated. In the process of honestly and courageously explaining to me and her support group how she had lost her old dreams, she found what she really needed. She found acceptance and caring.

Janet grew from a victim to a survivor and in the process found she had a special gift for forgiveness. She forgave more than anyone had a right to expect of her. This forgiveness removed much of the pain from her heart and left room for her to store love and happiness. She began to fall in love with her life.

The last time I spoke with Janet was four years after I had first met her. It was her wedding day. She told me she was in love, very happy, and glad to be alive.

Letting Go

Bitterness has a way of sticking to people. It can attach itself so strongly that the thought of letting it melt away can seem ridiculous. If we hold on to it long enough, we can start to rationalize its presence, convincing ourselves that we have a right to stay angry and that to do otherwise would be naive and foolish. Bitterness has a logic all its own, and it can be very persuasive in its argument. Once we allow it to enter our system, bitterness looks to move in. It does so by insisting that it only wants to protect us.

Bitterness, however, is like agoraphobia. An agoraphobic seeks safety by staying secluded in his home. To leave this shelter, he feels, would expose him to overwhelming danger. So he misses the opportunities and adventures life has to offer in order to maximize his security. Similarly, a bitter person will stay locked within her resentments in an attempt to protect herself from being hurt again. Like the agoraphobic, she will not be happy until she makes some changes. She will, however, be safe.

Locked behind their resentments, bitter people live insulated from human contact. Bitterness isolates those who carry it. It leaves them out in space on a cold, barren, desolate planet. No one likes this planet and no one would be there if they didn't feel they had to be. You see, when we are hurt by someone, besides dealing with the emotional upset, we are faced with a decision. We must decide whether or not we still want to live in a world where we can be hurt. Those who wish to remain in the human world must let go of their pain and bitterness. The others wind up on that cold and lonely planet. Here they stay until they let go of the hostility that sent them there.

The root meaning of the verb *to forgive* is to "let go."[3] Through forgiveness, we release pain that would otherwise fester within us. Forgiveness means letting go; it does not mean forgetting you were ever hurt. As psychotherapist Claudia Black says, "Forgiving is not forgetting. It is remembering and letting go."[4] We can hold on to a memory while letting go of the misery that originally accompanied it.

Even when we have the *right* to be angry, we do not *have* to be angry. Even when you've been hurt so badly that no one could blame you for carrying intense animosity, you can still rid yourself of the poison. The human capacity for forgiveness is beyond explanation. A recent news story, for instance, told of a mother who visited the state prison to tell her son's murderer that she had forgiven him. As a result, the mother and the murderer have become friends. I don't believe we can expect or demand this much forgiveness from people; it seems superhuman. It is, however, an example of the enormous potential humans have for forgiveness.

It should also be noted that this mother is not trying to get the murderer out of the penitentiary. He is capable of being homicidal and her forgiveness alone will not likely change this. She has not forgotten what he did. Her attitude toward him seems to be: "I forgive you for what you have done to me. I will not, however, help you hurt me or anyone else ever again." So she visits and maintains a friendship with her son's killer behind bars. She admits that before she had come to forgive this man, she had intense feelings of hatred toward him. It's probably fair to say she had every right to such feelings. Still, as if to prove that forgiveness is a miracle humans are capable of performing, she granted her own personal pardon which freed her from the hate.

We can release the pain of the past without repeating the past. We can protect ourselves without persecuting ourselves. Letting go of our resentments does not mean losing control of our lives. It may be an immense change, and change can be frightening, but no one ever died or went crazy or deteriorated in any way by forgiving someone.

Kin Hubbard quipped: "No one ever forgets where he buried the hatchet." It's not easy to let go of a hurt. After a time, if a resentment is not set free, it can become a person's focus. As time passes, the sore seems necessary. It's as if the void its absence would create might leave one completely empty. Carrying the hurt brings pain and frustration. But how can one be sure that this is worse than what may happen if one works through the spiritual surgery of forgiveness? In other words, sometimes forgiveness means dealing with the fear of facing the unknown.

Obviously, forgiveness can be difficult. It's complicated by the fact that resentments can be so deceiving. They can stick around long after you thought you had given them up. Psychotherapists have suggested that we can be fooled into a pseudo-forgiveness. Instead of actually letting go of the hurt, we hold on to it in our unconscious. We think we've put it behind us but we've really only put it in a backpack. There it may join other resentments. They may be *behind* us in the sense that we are not consciously aware of them, but we are still carrying them on our backs.

Putting bitterness in a backpack won't help. Unless this material comes back into awareness where it can be dealt with, it will continue to cause confusion. An individual with repressed resentments will experience intermittent, or perhaps continuous, feelings of anger, hostility, hurt, envy, or general discontent. He will find it difficult to act toward others in a caring way because his unconscious (i.e., his backpack) will grumble and punish anytime he becomes vunerable to more hurt. Consequently, he is more likely to stay guarded and protect his own territory. But because he has buried his hurt, he cannot explain (even to himself) why he feels the way he does. He cannot see what he has hidden from himself. But he can feel that something is wrong.

Until we are capable of letting go of our resentments, we will be tempted to hide them. Forgiveness is not a form of denial. We need to look good and hard at a hurt before we release it. Spiritual surgery, like all forms of surgery, has its pain. But it is a healthy pain in that it can be worked through. Furthermore, once the letting go is complete, a healthier person emerges. One with a straight back, a lighter heart, and a freer spirit. One who knows he is capable of forgiveness.

A person capable of forgiveness possesses the courage necessary for kindness. He can go out into the world, not immune from pain, but able to move beyond it. He spends less time protecting himself and more time giving of himself.

In the process of giving, new relationships are formed. We might call this the process of attaching ourselves to the Kindness Vine. It seems that even though forgiveness may mean letting go of certain relationships, it also means beginning new ones. Forgiveness can mean hello or it can mean good-bye. We may not be able to really detach ourselves from destructive relationships until we forgive those who hurt us. In this case, forgiveness would not mean returning to that harmful relationship; it would mean freeing ourselves so that we can reinvest ourselves in new, and hopefully healthier, relationships.

Sometimes forgiveness means settling old business in order to improve a relationship. Once you get beyond the hurt feelings, a relationship can get back on track and the parties involved can become reacquainted. At other times in your life forgiveness will mean letting go of a relationship altogether. The bitterness that kept you tied to the hurt will subside and you will find yourself free.

Letting go does not mean losing control. It does not mean blindly holding on to toxic relationships. On the contrary, when you forgive someone, you free yourself to choose if or how that person will fit into your life.

When you let go of hurt and resentment you become freer. When bitterness is removed from the heart, you are at once free to decide how you will fill the void. One of the most amazing phenomena performed by human nature occurs in the wake of forgiveness. After genuine forgiveness takes place, the void becomes a magnet for many valuable qualities. Notably, this void tends to attract serenity, gratitude, self-respect, and kindness.

In his book *Markings*, Dag Hammarskjold wrote, "Forgiveness is the answer to a child's dream of a miracle by which what was broken is made whole again, what is soiled is made clean." The void forgiveness leaves fills naturally. I won't pretend to know exactly how this works but I believe I have one important clue. Smedes calls forgiveness "spiritual surgery." Hammarskjold likened it to "a miracle." This, I think, is more than rhetoric. Forgiveness is a spiritual process that offers powerful spiritual rewards. Forgiveness provides the spirit with room to grow. As it grows, the spirit becomes stronger.

The most striking feature of those I have known who have carried hurt and resentment and then learned to let it go is their awakened spirituality. This is my clue about the nature of forgiveness. It leads people to consider their connectedness with a larger universe, one that is centered on caring rather than selfishness. The bitterness is replaced by a warmth that is contagious because it seeks to be shared. Forgiveness does not take you back to the person you were before you were hurt. It takes you to a much higher plane.

People will feel safe to be around you. They know they can be themselves with someone capable of forgiveness. If you can forgive, you will be much more likely to thrive in an imperfect world. It will be *your* world and you will feel the responsibility and desire to contribute to it.

Forgiveness can turn a person's life around. It has tremendous power. It should be made clear, however, that forgiveness has its limitations. Your forgiveness may never change the person who hurt you. Beyond this, a hurt can take time to heal, sometimes a long time. Forgiveness has its limitations. But if we understand and accept these limitations, then we will know its real power.

What Forgiveness Cannot Do

In the process of forgiving someone, there arises a tendency to want to help that person. This is an indication of the kindness that accompanies forgiveness. But what confuses many of us is the reality that even after we have pardoned someone, they may continue to try to hurt us. Our absolution does not necessarily turn sinners into saints. It frees us only from the emotional chains that link us to the hurt. This leaves us with a clearer head to decide whom we will love and trust. Forgiveness changes the one who forgives, but not always the forgiven.

One of the best stories ever told about the nature of forgiveness was written long ago by Fyodor Dostoevsky. In *The Brothers Karamazov* he tells of a very wicked woman who died without repenting.

Once upon a time, according to Dostoyevsky, there lived a heartless woman. So evil was she that no one could recall her performing a single kind act. When the woman died, she quickly met the devil, who plunged her deep into hell, what Dostoevsky described as the "lake of fire." Her guardian angel, however, would not give up on this soul. The angel thought and thought in an effort to remember a good deed performed by the woman. He wanted to tell God of such a deed in the hope that He might remove the woman from hell. Finally, the angel recalled such an incident and hurried to inform God.

"She once pulled up an onion in her garden and gave it to a beggar woman," said the angel.

"You take that onion then," answered God, "hold it out to her in the lake, and then let her take hold and be pulled out. And if you can pull her out of the lake, let her come to paradise, but if the onion breaks, then the woman must stay where she is."

So the angel rushed to the woman and cried, "Come, catch hold and I will pull you out."

The woman followed the angel's instructions and the angel began pulling her out of the fire. Just as she was being lifted above the flames, the other inhabitants of hell, seeing her escape, began grabbing hold of her so that they too would be released. But in keeping with her wicked ways, she started kicking them and shouted: "I am to be pulled out, not you! It's my onion, not yours!" With these words the onion broke. The woman fell back into the lake of fire where—so the story goes —"She is burning to this day."

"So the angel wept and went away," wrote Dostoevsky.

The angel grieved. He had held out an onion to no avail. I bet he tried to help her be a good person throughout her life. And every time she did something mean he would forgive her. But she never changed. If we are to believe Dostoevsky, not even God's forgiveness could change her.

Forgiveness means you let go of your hurt. As the pain leaves you, you realize that any desire to hurt others has gone too. Forgiveness removes the desire to be spiteful. It will not, however, necessarily make others more caring. Your forgiveness may seem miraculous to you, but it may be meaningless to the one you have forgiven. If you can accept this, you can forgive.

If you do not carry hurt within you, you are less likely to distribute it to others. No one needs to carry this load.

Forgiveness is not a perfect process. It doesn't make the world fair or just. Another one of its limitations is the time it takes. Sometimes the key ingredient in forgiveness is time. We need to recognize where it hurts and then make the appropriate repairs. Anger is entitled to have its day. We must touch a feeling and then hold it before we can let it go. Letting go does not mean avoiding. It means releasing that which was once held.

Forgiveness can take time. It deserves the time it needs. How long it takes to forgive depends on the people and events involved. Unfortunately, it can be hard to distinguish between *time to hurt* and *time to heal*. Identifying the point where forgiveness can and should begin is not always easy. It can require some soul-searching.

Will Rogers recommended that we not let yesterday use up too much of today. Maybe this is the point where forgiveness should begin, the point when yesterday starts using up too much of today. Maybe this is the point when we start to feel the voice that says it's time to start letting go. Here the hurting gives way to healing.

Forgiveness can take time, sometimes a lot of time, and it doesn't make the world perfect. These two flaws alone can lead one to wonder if it's worth the effort. Whether or not forgiveness is "worth it" probably depends more than anything on how much we want to *use* today. Those who invest their energies in the present live healthier, happier, and more compassionate lives. They love their lives.

People who have worked to become forgivers will tell you it's worth it. Those who have not may suggest otherwise.

A Forgiving Nature

Once you have felt forgiveness, it can become a part of your character. If you live a full life and reach out to many people, there will be opportunities to forgive. Forgiveness is a necessary survival skill in an imperfect world, especially if you live your life to the fullest.

The kindest people I have ever known have all had something in common. They have all understood that people have faults. Beyond this, they accept imperfect people. It's as if they are prepared to forgive because they know that the need to forgive will surely arise again. This is not a pessimistic attitude.

Indeed, it is profoundly optimistic. A human being with a forgiving way can survive and thrive in a world that sometimes hurts.

In his book *Love Is Letting Go of Fear,* Gerald G. Jampolsky writes: "The unforgiving mind, contrasted with the forgiving mind, is confused, afraid and full of fear." Not convinced of its ability to survive, the unforgiving mind doubts its ability to function properly. It protects itself by isolating itself, often behind walls of hostility or indifference. Should the mind decide to start forgiving, the walls come down. As the walls disappear, the fear and confusion wane. In some respects, this is the point where one's spiritual life blossoms. Here one feels in harmony with a vast universe. It's the sense of true belonging and contentment. Maybe Jampolsky was right when he said that "forgiveness is the key to happiness."

We actualize the full power of forgiveness when it becomes a way of life for us and not just a technique for correcting a single event. There lies a large ocean between "I can forgive" and "I do forgive." Occasional reminders that "I can forgive" point to one's potential for crossing that ocean and living in the place where "I do forgive." Maybe this is the place folks are looking for when we say we want to find happiness.

A forgiving nature is not something that can be bought, stolen, or passed on in twenty-five words or less. It is an attitude that refuses to let us hold on to the hurts of the past. It is the belief that people can change and often do. It is also a commitment to let today be today, free from the grudges that belonged to yesterday.

It isn't always easy, though. As we have noted, some hurts take time to heal and they deserve time. We will end this chapter with a piece of advice on how to move on when you feel stuck. It is a suggestion that sounds incredible to a lot of people when they first hear it, yet it is a suggestion that I have seen help many.

The following passage comes from the book *Alcoholics Anonymous* or what members of AA call "the Big Book." In the chapter entitled "Freedom from Bondage," you can find these words:

> If you have a resentment you want to be free of, if you will pray for the person or thing that you resent, you will be free. If you will ask in prayer for everything you want for yourself to be given to them, you will be free. Ask for their health, their prosperity, their happiness, and you will be free. Even when you don't really want it for them, and your prayers are only words and you don't mean it, go ahead and do it anyway. Do it every day for two weeks and you will find you have come to mean it and to want it for them, and you will realize that where you used to feel bitterness and resentment and hatred, you now feel compassionate understanding and love.

I'm not sure how the time period of two weeks was reached, but it's not etched in stone. It may take more time for some. It's important to keep in mind that forgiveness allows for time to heal.

AA recommends prayer to help us learn to forgive. But they certainly aren't the only ones to make this type of connection. Lewis B. Smedes, author of *Forgive and Forget*, made this observation: "When we forgive we come as close as any human can to the essentially divine act of creation. . . . When we forgive . . . we walk in stride with God. And we heal the hurt we never deserved."

Smedes, Alcoholics Anonymous, as well as many others who have examined this topic, point to the spiritual aspect of forgiveness. It seems they are all giving similar counsel. Sometimes a hurt can be just too heavy to lift. When you let it go, it stays put, unwilling or unable to roll away in spite of your best individual efforts. In these instances, we need the hurt to be lifted by a force more powerful than ourselves.

6

HEALING

In truth, giving is not just a natural act; when
our cup runneth over, it hurts *not* to give.
We see the pain in another, and, knowing the balm
for the pain, we want to ease the hurting.
                    John-Roger and Peter McWilliams
                    Life 101

Kindness heals. It heals the body, the mind, and the spirit.
It is the common thread that runs through all forms of
healing.

I won't suggest that kindness is a magic cure that, by itself,
can mend any wound. It's not that easy. Healers who treat the
body, mind, or spirit all have their own special strategies and
techniques. They must respect a unique set of laws that pertain
to their particular specialties. It can take years to gain the
knowledge required to make certain types of repairs. We are
complex beings with countless varieties of infirmity. To reduce
healing to a single dimension would be foolish. It would be
equally absurd, however, to overlook what may be *the* essential
ingredient in mending wounded human beings.

But this is more than just a chapter on the relationship
between kindness and healing. It is also a chapter about power.
Kindness has power, real power. It is more than a courtesy. It
is a force that heals and creates. It not only improves the

quality of life; studies have shown that kindness keeps people living longer.

Caring cures ailments of the mind, body, and spirit. It's a medication that anyone can prescribe—anyone who can handle its power. But here's the catch. The power can be frightening. We are capable of achieving more personal power than most of us ever know. We can be reluctant to touch the power within us for fear that it may place demands on us. Actualizing our power to heal, for instance, may drive us to serve others. Denying this force keeps us on our own island, perhaps safe, but without the mission that life rewards us with when we open our gifts and put our talents in motion.

Erich Fromm once remarked that most of us die before we are fully born. Many of us go through our lives without ever touching the power within. Human beings have genuine healing power. Much of this power comes through simple kindnesses. I'm afraid we overlook the power in kindness. But it's there. In fact, kindness may be humankind's most effective means of healing.

In his book *Principles of Internal Medicine,* physician Tinsley Randolph Harrison wrote, "In the treatment of suffering, there is a need for technical skill, scientific knowledge and human understanding." Human understanding is a necessary quality in the healing process. Scientific knowledge and technical skill alone are enough to fix robots. People require a dose of compassion. This is what separates mechanics from healers—the compassion.

My father, a small-town doctor, had a sense of this. Starting when we were little (i.e., around age three), he would take me or one of my brothers and sisters along with him on house calls. He thought that small children were good for old, sickly shut-ins. And by all indications, he was right. I can remember walking into these patients' homes. At first, they always appeared to be at death's door. But I can't recall a single old person who didn't make a fuss as soon as he or she saw us. They would, almost without exception, get out of bed or off the couch and start moving. The men usually began bouncing their fists, playfully inviting me to box with them. The women, on the other hand, hugged and offered food, most often juice and "saltines." I can still see the energy fill them as we walked in. And they almost always laughed.

After the patients had a few minutes with me, I would wait in the living room or on the porch while the examination took place. Then it was on to the next house for more saltines and boxing.

Today there are "experimental" programs in certain nursing homes that resemble my early house calls. The research is noting the positive impact caring for puppies, kittens, and plants can have on the elderly. They live longer, healthier, and happier lives. Not only do they feel productive, they also feel the health that comes from caring. They also feel the incalculable rewards that come from being needed and being cared for in return.

Giving and receiving kindness are both tremendously therapeutic forces. Environments that encourage either foster health. But those extraordinary contexts that provide opportunities for both giving and receiving kindness are places where healing abounds. Kindness contains a healing force, a force too potent and unique to measure precisely.

Ernest Hemingway wrote, "The world breaks everyone and afterward some are strong at the broken places." It's true that we need different treatments for different troubles. It's also true that there are similarities among us in how we mend. Healing is a science and an art. There are reasons why some become strong in the broken places.

Healing is a journey that cannot always be traveled alone. Someone once said that misery loves company. Well, this isn't really true. Misery lives in loneliness. Healing, however, usually involves a transplant of some kind. On occasion, the transplant is the bodily type such as a heart or a kidney. More often, the transplant is of the spiritual or psychological variety such as courage, hope, humor, or compassion. Sometimes solitude can provide the needed transplant. While taking time to be alone, a soul can find what it needs. The transplants donated by solitude can be so personal that they cannot be put accurately into words. Solitude has its own special curative powers. Conversations with solitude can be good for your mind and spirit.

"Doctors who persist in thinking they can cure disease without caring for the person may be excellent technicians," wrote surgeon and bestselling author Bernie S. Siegel, "but they are incomplete doctors, because they have an incomplete understanding of illness."[1] Following this line of thought, we might conclude that caring is a necessary transplant in the effort to cure any disease.

Sigmund Freud once remarked to Carl Jung that his own method of treatment—psychoanalysis—was "in essence a cure through love." Freud, a man not prone to sentiment, knew that people are more than just analyzable psyches. He has been, for the most part, remembered as the genius who dissected the mind and made psychotherapy a science. But he was well aware of the human need for caring as well as the devastating effects of a life without love.

Years later, in an effort to understand the medical consequences of loneliness, psychologist James J. Lynch conducted a thorough study on how human contact and companionship impact one's physical health. His research concluded that the lack of human companionship, the sudden loss of love, and chronic human loneliness are significant contributors to serious disease (including cardiovascular disease) and premature death.[2] We don't do well alone. There's something life-giving in human contact. Even solitude has more power when there is someone waiting for us when we return from the quiet.

Giving and receiving kindness and caring are beneficial to our bodies. The research data to support this continue to grow. Another important study followed several thousand people over a ten-year period and found that individuals who do regular volunteer work show a dramatic increase in life expectancy over those who perform no such service for others.[3] It seems that those who make a habit of and commitment to helping others live longer.

It's simple. Caring is good for you. Besides proving beneficial to your body, it also improves your psychological and emotional functioning. Prominent contemporary psychologist Martin Seligman, for instance, insists that depression stems partly from an overcommitment to the self and an undercommitment to the common good.[4] I can't take good care of me unless I spend some time taking care of you. And I cannot take good care of you unless I take care of me. What all this comes down to is—our needs fit together.

Seligman is by no means the first or only scholar to point to the psychological benefits of altruism. Years ago, Alfred Adler argued that we cannot achieve genuine mental health until we develop what he called "social interest." Social interest is a drive to work toward the common good of humankind. Unless we find this desire, we will never be fulfilled.

Social interest became a central tenet in Adlerian psychology. He believed wholeheartedly that if one is to help build a person's character and feelings of worth, one must stimulate that person's kindness and generosity. When we extend ourselves to help others, Adler believed, we become personally gratified and empowered.[5] Altruism, we are learning, is an effective treatment for depression and anxiety. It builds self-confidence and courage. It also serves as a remedy for chronic anger and hostility. In my career I have worked with many hostile individuals, and I have never ceased to be amazed by how many of these people, who appear to be looking everywhere for a fight, are really desperately searching for kindness. So often their animosity is the result of not finding the caring they need.

Julius Segal, another psychologist who has written eloquently about the healing powers of compassion, maintained that caring can be necessary in the treatment of bereavement.

According to Segal, the pain we feel, the losses we sustain, become infinitely more bearable when we adopt a mission of caring.[6] Thus we see the power in support groups such as those that help the grief-stricken. In these marvelous communities, suffering souls help themselves by helping each other. There may be nothing more therapeutic and growth-enhancing than a mission of caring. Where it exists, there is health and healing.

Take, for instance, an example used by Segal. When the American hostages were released from Iran in 1981, they were immediately taken to an American military hospital in Weisbaden, Germany. On their first morning there, they began their healing process by getting together as a group to decide on a message to send to the families of the helicopter pilots who were shot down and killed in the rescue attempt. Next, they gathered the sea of gifts that poured in from around the world. (Companies from everywhere sent them everything from candy bars to china in celebration of their return.) They then loaded the gifts on carts and distributed them to the sick people in the hospital.[7]

To the best of my knowledge, no one told the former hostages to make the welfare of others their first concern. Their knack for health guided them along this path. The most therapeutic procedure this hospital had to offer the hostages may have been the opportunity for kindness. Healthy people help people. While they were hostages they may have been deprived (due to their isolation) of the ability to exercise their compassion. Once freed, however, this healthy need moved to be acted upon. The hospital should be congratulated for allowing this behavior to blossom again.

It should be noted that we can imprison ourselves. By this I mean we can deprive ourselves of opportunities for kindness. In so doing, we lose our vitality. When we imprison ourselves, we make it difficult for someone to come and rescue us. We have to start rescuing ourselves. We rescue ourselves through compassion and generosity. The spirit within each of us (if we give it the opportunity) lives compassionately. It can thrive only in a person willing to live a life of concern and caring for others. Without compassion, the spirit withers.

When the spirit weakens, the mind and body tend to follow. It's hard to feel healthy and think clearly when one lacks a mission in life. The spirit provides this sense of mission. It answers the question: what am I to do with my life? The spirit is our source of enthusiasm and appreciation for life. It moves us. It builds us. It carries us. And sometimes, when we need it, it can cure us.

We live in an age when people are coming to understand the healing power of the spirit. We are not yet at the point where we feel comfortable speaking openly about this. Instead we prefer to read about it. During the past few years or so, many popular books have carried the message of what is sometimes called holistic health—an approach toward health that includes the body, mind, and spirit. The great demand for these books indicates a high level of interest in this area. Even so, it seems folks would rather read about it than talk about it. Maybe it's still too embarrassing to say out loud, "I think there's a spiritual dimension to healing."

The spiritual dimension of healing is not so much overlooked as it is avoided. We see it and feel it, but we frequently try to call it something else. We may admire people who talk about it, but it's difficult to do so ourselves. It's important to realize this because there are probably times in all of our lives when we feel frustrated by not knowing how to help someone we care about. At the core of this frustration is that person's unwillingness to admit that his or her spirit hurts.

I once heard someone explain that physicians have it easier than veterinarians because human patients can report the location and severity of their pain whereas animals cannot. Well, this isn't quite true. Struggling, suffering people many times cannot tell you where it hurts either. Sometimes the thought of exposing one's spirituality is, for whatever reason, too threatening. Other people just don't have the words to describe a spiritual wound. We can't rely solely on verbal communication in our efforts to help others heal. At times we have to provide a courage transplant or even a vocabulary transplant in order to help someone identify a spiritual need. In any case, when attempting to help someone heal, we are wise to approach him aware that the spirit is an essential force in all types of recovery.

When my father took me on house calls, he had two rules we always tried to follow. First, touch the person. Most often this was a handshake but, at the same time, it was more than a handshake. You see, you were not to let go until it was time. Knowing how long to hold on usually had nothing to do with what the patient may have said. Instead, you held on as long as that person's hand needed it. The hand told you. And if you listened, you knew.

Second, always look for opportunities for humor. Spontaneity was great but sometimes we even rehearsed a line or two before entering the house. It didn't take long for me to learn what an effective medicine humor is. Making someone, especially a sick person, laugh may be only a small act of kindness. But there is power in these tiny deeds. If you feel enough of these deeds, you will come to understand these lines of William Wordsworth:

> The best portion of a good man's life,
> His little, nameless, unremembered acts
> Of kindness and love.

Handshakes and humor are both ways of touching someone. Interestingly, both these simple acts touch the body, the emotions, and the spirit. It would be hard to overstate their importance. Now (as an adult) I have come to learn that there is a third equally simple, yet equally important, ingredient in the healing process—listening.

As I said, people are like animals in the sense that we can't always say where it hurts. Sometimes we stumble, fumble, and stutter before we find the courage and the words we need. This can take time.

Listening is an act of kindness with awesome therapeutic power. Even if you cannot offer a solution, you can offer your presence. Many times a supportive ear is more beneficial in the long run than a solution.

In *Out of Solitude*, Henri Nouwen wrote:

> The friend who can be silent with us in a moment of despair or confusion, who can stay with us in an hour of grief and bereavement, who can tolerate not-knowing, not-curing, not-healing, and face with us the reality of our powerlessness, that is a friend who cares.

The word *compassion* comes from a Latin root meaning, literally, "to suffer with." Just having someone there with you in times of need can be more than comforting. Having someone to talk to and be with can mean the difference between life and death. When we give or receive kindness, we are reminded that life is worth living. With this awareness, we become a little more invincible.

Shakespeare penned in *Macbeth*, "Give sorrow words; the grief that does not speak whispers the o'erfraught heart and bids it break." Words come, though perhaps painfully at first, when there is a caring ear to receive and respect them. Sometimes courage arises as soon as someone really hears you say, "I'm scared." Hope can also arrive in the silence of a good listener.

Feeling understood is much like the feeling of being loved. When human beings feel loved, we have an almost automatic reaction to give love in return. Receiving love works like a heart transplant. Once it is received, it works for the recipient in the same way it worked for the donor. With this type of transplant, however, there should never be a shortage of donors.

We are coming to understand what the poets knew long ago, that love and caring are healing forces. We can transplant courage, hope, enthusiasm, humor, and love. Some people receive their transplants through poetry, the Bible, or an inspiring passage. Others find their donor in a friend, a nurse, a doctor, or a child. The common trait in all these donors is a genuine desire to help. It's people who care who transplant health.

Medical research over the past sixty years has repeatedly shown that a warm, caring touch stimulates growth and physical health in children just as withholding normal human contact and physical affection leads to physical and emotional deterioration.[8] The body and spirit need to be cared for and not just taken care of. Children who are fed and sheltered in uncaring environments grow weak in all areas of their beings. They never develop the strength to deal with life. Some become so cynical that they refuse to believe that anyone is really capable of caring for anything. Fearing more hurt and rejection, they seal themselves off from attempts to rescue them. I have seen children as young as eight years old who seem to have given up on kindness. To them, caring is just a manipulation. They won't let it in and, consequently, they deny themselves the caring they need.

We are all capable of refusing a cure. It has been said that the door to the human heart can be opened only from the inside. Maybe it's true that the best we can do is invite someone to open the door. If they decline the invitation, then we may not be able to do much more than leave something at their doorway. Then, should they ever open the door, they will have something to reach out for.

Before people will receive kindness, they need to know that it's safe to open their doors. Often the first step toward helping people is convincing them you won't hurt them. Once this is accomplished, people move to accept the power of compassion. At this point, with the heart open, we are capable of expressing what's inside. These are the early stages of healing.

Caring and compassion have extraordinary healing powers. These powers can benefit anyone willing to receive them. They can also be used to help us help ourselves.

Healing Ourselves

Just as we are capable of hurting ourselves, we also have power to help heal ourselves. We can mend our bodies, settle our minds, and lift our spirits. We tend to know ourselves better than anyone else does. We know what makes us feel better and what doesn't. Even when we can't put it into words, we know where it hurts. Furthermore, we know, better than anyone else, when we are ready to let go of pain and when we are really set to take the steps necessary to heal.

Healing ourselves means caring for ourselves, a process not always as easy as it might sound. Caring for ourselves is so often confused with selfishness that many people feel guilty about showing themselves kindness. These folks hang on to the irrational belief that good people don't need vacations or that only stingy people buy themselves presents. Well, this isn't true at all. We need to care for ourselves. Idle hands are *not* always the devil's workshop. It's O.K. to take that nap you've been promising yourself. Looking in the mirror and complimenting yourself does not mean you're conceited. And saying aloud words to encourage yourself will not make you crazy.

We've created so many reasons not to give ourselves what we need that it may seem that caring for ourselves indicates a character flaw. This myth needs to go. We have every right to address our own needs. Caring for ourselves does not kill our desire or ability to care for others. On the contrary, it enhances our capacity for altruism.

Dr. Seuss was right when he claimed that "Life's a Great Balancing Act."[9] With all the best intentions at heart we can still tilt the scales and become unbalanced. We need to balance what we give with what we have. A healthy, rested, energetic person has much more to share than one who has driven oneself to exhaustion or even death.

Through his work with cancer patients, surgeon Bernie Siegel came to see how caring *only* for others can be deleterious to one's own health. "Over and over again I heard friends and relatives (of cancer victims) say, 'He was a saint. Why him?' The truth is that compulsively proper and generous people predominate among cancer patients because they put the needs of others ahead of their own."[10] Dr. Siegel's warning echoes Dr. Seuss's advice about life being a Great Balancing Act. The healthiest among us find a way to care for others as well as themselves. They don't decide between "either/or" nor do they put one ahead of the other. Caring for others coexists with caring for themselves.

There are reasons why some people care for others more than themselves. One of the most common explanations is the fact that there are those who feel others' distress more intensely than their own.[11] When we stop listening to ourselves, we suffer the consequences of neglect. The body uses what devices it has—often physical or mental illness—to call attention to its needs. Unfortunately, by the time we hear it, the damage may already have been done.

It's not surprising that this situation occurs so frequently. If we really allow ourselves to experience the world around us, the cries for help can be deafening. A caring heart in this needy world can be overwhelmed. The troubles of others can seem so much more legitimate than our own. It can reach a point where we can lose touch with our own signals and push onward even while running below empty.

When it's all said and done, what we are talking about here is humility. We all need kindness. We all need healing at times. Caretakers (including the best and most dedicated) are not exempt from this. We have to accept the fact that we have a limited amount of energy and resources. We need to be replenished. You have to be alive and focused to work on your mission. Little hurts become bigger when they are not allowed to heal. You have to abide by the rules of life. This means that people who neglect themselves end up wishing they hadn't. Caring for yourself can be difficult. We become caught up in the fear that a love of self is selfish or egocentric. Consequently, we can feel guilty about loving ourselves and loving our lives.

This is an irrational guilt. Loving ourselves is an important part in the process of loving humanity. If we don't care for the caretakers, there may one day be no caretakers left. No one comes into the world with a maintenance-free guarantee. We all need some work and we are entitled to the right to work on ourselves.

There's a story I like about two painters on their lunch break. One of them looks into his lunchbox and protests, "Peanut butter, peanut butter, peanut butter! I hate peanut butter! I can't take another day of it!"

His partner inquires, "Why don't you ask your wife to make you something else?"

"Oh, I'm not married," replies the first. "I make my own lunch."[12]

It's often just as easy to make ourselves something we like as it is to prepare something we don't. But we become misdirected by those irrational beliefs that forbid us from paying ourselves the attention we deserve. Being good to ourselves is not necessarily the same thing as selfishness or self-indulgence. Selfish people care *only* for themselves. Healthy people tend to their own needs and then use their energy and means to serve the universe.

Self-care is necessary for health. But alone it does not provide one with an adequate mission in life. To know a genuine, deep sense of purpose, we must care for others. In the course of this mission of caring, we will be called to sacrifice. This means that our kindness may, in some ways, cost us. So be it. Many of us are called on to make sacrifices; few of us are called on to be martyrs. Few of us are called on to die for our convictions, but we are *all* called to *live* for our sacred beliefs.

If we care for ourselves, we have much more to give. Without strength, people are not prone to sacrifice.

I realize that the written word has only so much power. Convincing you that you deserve to be cared for by you can take a while. I have experienced the frustration of trying to persuade certain people that it's all right to treat themselves. The problem with selfish individuals is that they don't care enough for other people. The trouble with certain altruists is that they won't move to help themselves. Both groups make the mistake of concluding that we have to decide between me or them. They do not see the potential for harmony or balance. But it's there. Your needs and the needs of nature and humanity are quite compatible.

Several years ago I attended an assertiveness-training workshop that was facilitated by a colleague. Although I had never been to this type of class before, the first half hour or so went pretty much as I had expected. Then something interesting and unforeseen occurred. My friend began to tell the participants about self-esteem and how and why it can deteriorate. One of the most common reasons behind a poor self-concept, he told them, is that people refuse to accept compliments. When praised for doing good work, for instance, instead of saying, "Thank you. That means a lot to me coming from you," they simply scoff, shrug it off, and if they say anything at all it's something like, "It's nothing."

The truth can have a way of making you laugh, and when I heard this, I started to chuckle. I agreed immediately with my friend's point. If we let kind words in, not only will our self-esteem be healthier, we will probably have more kindness inside us. But here again we run into irrational notions. "It's vain to take compliments seriously," or "Nobody really means a compliment anyway; it's just something you're supposed to say," or "Praise is just a cheap form of manipulation."

Earlier I talked about how kindness is contagious and how it spreads from one person to another. An exception to this rule arises when we refuse to see or accept the kindness that is right in front of us. This blindness is usually caused by one of the most destructive, mistaken beliefs of all: "I don't deserve kindness." Once someone reaches this conclusion, life becomes bitter and heartless. One feels cut off and alone.

Those caught in this faulty belief system need to change their thinking and allow themselves to receive care, both from themselves and others. They need to understand that *everyone deserves kindness.*

If you will not accept kindness, you will miss what life has to offer. We may not have the right to demand that anyone love or care for us. It's wonderful when it happens, but we cannot control its arrival. The only kindness and respect that we can control is the kindness and respect we give ourselves. Once this is in place, though, we begin to open ourselves to receive whatever love and caring may be offered to us.

It's easier being kind to yourself if you've had a good teacher, someone who, for instance, took the time to appreciate beauty, took a sick day when needed, or spent some time alone reading good books, sitting in a hot tub, or going for walks. If you've had the opportunity to know people who have been kind to themselves, you have a head start. All in all, however, a teacher is not absolutely essential. All you really need to do is make a decision that you deserve to receive kindness from you.

Although people frequently say things like, "I would love to spend some time taking care of me, but I just don't have the time," the fact is that time has little to do with it. It's not that we can't; it's that we won't. It doesn't take a long time to compliment yourself. (But if you think this is conceited, you might feel guilty.) And you can certainly slow down for a few minutes to watch the sun set. (Unless, of course, you think only lunatics do this and then you might be embarrassed.) Being kind to yourself is usually free. But you can afford it only if you have given yourself enough freedom and respect.

There are countless ways to be kind to yourself and we could spend forever discussing the merits of this practice. It is not my intention, however, to preach or force this decision upon anyone. My hope here is to raise the issue in your mind and leave you to decide what you shall do with it. But before we move on, I would like to briefly describe three commonly overlooked dimensions of being good to yourself. These are:

1. Be good to your conscience.
2. Listen to yourself (and be willing to act on what you hear).
3. Be grateful.

Be good to your conscience. The human conscience has long been the victim of a bad rap. Instead of seeing it as the guide that it is, we tend to think of it as an overbearing disciplinarian ready to pounce at the first sign that we are about to step out of line. We've come to see it as the Dirty Harry of our psyches whose sole purpose is to catch us in the act and then flog us relentlessly.

A good relationship between a person and his conscience is generally thought to be one where the person obeys his or her conscience. If you just listen and obey, all will be fine. Well, this myth is completely erroneous. Your conscience does not want you to be a child and it most certainly has no interest in being your parent or nanny. It will, however, accept the role of friend, guide, or confidant.

It's not enough to listen to your conscience; you have to talk to it. A conscience will suffer when left alone. It needs to be integrated into your being. Your conscience is the part of you that collects what you've been taught about what is right. It contains a good portion of your history, your roots, and your character. Turning away from it means turning away from who you are. If you neglect your conscience, besides the guilt, you will feel confusion about your own identity.

A good conscience is a priceless gift. Realize this. A good conscience may, in fact, be the most expensive item in the world. It has kept you from stealing everything you ever wanted. It pushes you to make donations even when the rest of you grabs for the security of some extra money in your pocket. Indeed, a healthy conscience may not make good business sense. But it does make good human sense.

In order to be truly happy, you need to invite your conscience into your being. Learn to recognize its voice and speak to it enough that it recognizes yours. Listen when it congratulates you for the sacrifices you've made for someone else. Speak to it of the beliefs you've chosen. If it never hears your own words, it tends to fill with the ideas of others.

Set aside some time to dialogue with your conscience. Give it a face, if this helps you come to know it better. Then understand that this face is capable of expressing profound emotions such as sorrow, joy, anguish, elation, despair, anger, hope, and gratitude. This dialogue will allow you to find harmony. After all, your conscience does not seek obedience; it hopes for harmony.

If you can find and recognize your conscience, respect it, listen to it, share yourself with it, and then you will know serenity. Within this serenity lies much power for healing your hurts.

Listen to yourself (and be willing to act on what you hear). The fact that our ears are on the outside of our bodies can be misleading. You see, too many people come to the conclusion that listening occurs only between a person and his environment. Such is not the case. Some of the most important listening we can ever do takes place *within* ourselves. It's here that, if we listen carefully, we learn when we need to laugh, cry, grieve, create, ask, mend, and get up to try again. The only way we have of knowing what we need is by listening to ourselves.

Sad to say, some folks don't know even their own language. On occasion, they hear something screaming from within themselves, but because they have not spent enough time listening and learning their own tongue, they are unable to interpret what they hear. Spiritual needs become confused with bodily needs. Emotional needs become confused with spiritual needs. A spiritual need, misunderstood and unanswered, can turn into physical pain. An unresolved psychological conflict can lead to spiritual deprivation. People can blame God for their own unfinished business. If we don't listen to the voices within us, we won't know how to give ourselves what we need.

People are more likely to heal if they feel heard. Children, for instance, start to feel better as soon as someone understands how their skinned knees hurt. Adults are more likely to resume a job search after hearing that someone else understands what it's like to be out of work. And if there's one characteristic held in common by every atheist I've ever known, it's the belief that he or she is not being heard. Consequently, you probably won't convince many atheists of the existence of God by *arguing* with them. Instead, they are more likely to open themselves to the existence of God if you *listen* to them.

Prayer makes sense only if there is a God who will listen. To those who believe that no one hears them, the spirit has very little power, enthusiasm, or direction. We need to be heard. But before we can ask God or anyone else to hear us, we need to listen to ourselves. Only then will we know what we need, and then what we need to say.

I've always felt that God is a very good listener. I've never heard anyone say that He's interrupted them or cut them off. Coincidentally or not, listening is a vital ingredient in healing. It is a technique we can use to care for ourselves. You deserve to be heard. You deserve your own attention. You're worth listening to.

When people sense they are being heard, they feel valued. If we are to value ourselves, we must listen to ourselves. Spend some time alone in a place where you can hear yourself. Write down your thoughts and feelings if it helps you to access and remember them. Allow yourself to be surprised by what you hear. If you do, you will be more likely to hear the truth.

Some may tell you that attending to yourself is just another form of selfishness. Be cautious of such advice. Certain people would rather have you listen to them because controlling you becomes much easier if you will not hear your own inner voice. Once your inner voice is silenced or neglected, you become quite vulnerable to manipulation.

You need to spend some time caring for yourself. Unless you listen to yourself, you won't know how. Make friends with yourself. Listen to that part of you that can identify what you need. Value yourself enough to care for yourself. Be kind to yourself.

Be grateful. In the final chapter, we will address the relationship between gratitude and generosity. The relationship is a simple yet extremely important one. Genuine generosity is rooted in gratitude. As long as the gratitude stays alive, the urge to contribute will thrive. Once the thankfulness disappears, however, generosity tends to vanish.

I'm afraid that expressing gratitude is a skill too few of us ever learn. We let the gratitude we feel sit silently until we lose touch with it. It's as if we are waiting for permission to be grateful.

Some of us have been fortunate enough to have had effective role models in this area. A few years ago, for example, I was lucky enough to meet Elizabeth. In her late fifties, Elizabeth was a recovering alcoholic who had dedicated her life toward helping other female addicts get into recovery. She had also become one of the happiest people I had ever known.

One of the most important lessons I learned from Elizabeth involved gratitude. In spite of a life filled with pain and heartache, she was very grateful for all the good things she had been given. Perhaps more than anyone I have ever known, she had learned to appreciate, *really appreciate,* her blessings, however small or seemingly insignificant to others. Above everything else, she was thankful for being alive. On several occasions during her drinking years, she came close to death but always managed to pull through. I once told her that she was a member of "The Lucky to Be Alive Club." She laughed, agreed, and then thanked me.

Elizabeth had learned an important bit of wisdom. She knew we all need to express our gratitude. Her gratitude for her life was constantly being communicated. As kind and caring as a person can be, she turned her life into one big thank-you. It wasn't unusual at all for her (during an attack of thankfulness) to lift her eyes to the heavens and exclaim, "Thank You, God!" More than anything, Elizabeth taught me about the relationship between gratitude and happiness. It is a close one. The happiest people alive, it seems, are those with the longest gratitude lists. They notice and remember the positives that come their way. It's not that they have more good fortune, of course, it's that they are aware of and grateful for what they have. I once heard someone say that Elizabeth had had "a bad life." But it would have taken her forever to describe all she had been given.

As long as you are alive, you have something to be grateful for. The question is: do you see it? Or are you too preoccupied with your wish list to consider a gratitude list?

If you seek mental health and happiness, tend to your gratitude list. If you are alive, you have enough to start a potent list. Include specifics and generalities. Include those things that you know belong, even though they might not make sense to anyone else. Use your courage to include everything that belongs on your list and then keep adding to it.

If you develop an attitude of gratitude, your colors will become brighter, your relationships will run deeper, and the music you hear will become more powerful. You create the good life by being grateful for the one you have.

Be good to your conscience. Listen to yourself. Be grateful. Understand that you have a right and a need to care for yourself. The motivation for healthy self-care grows out of humility. Through humility we see and accept our limitations and our needs. This vision and acceptance is part of health and healing. It would be vain and self-centered to expect others to satisfy all our needs. We must be willing to address some of our own.

Selfishness sets in when we forget about that Great Balancing Act. We have to consider and address *both* our own needs
and the needs of those around us. If we deal with only one end
of the scale, we become unbalanced. We also have to accept
the fact that we cannot meet all our own needs. We can't give
ourselves all the kindness we need. We can't scratch our own
backs. Complimenting ourselves doesn't always do the trick.
Now and then it's nice to hear someone else's opinion. It feels
good to make ourselves feel better, but we'll never feel really
good if our efforts are aimed *only* at assisting ourselves. In order
to live at peace in the forest, we have to tend to all the life
forms.

While loving and caring for yourself will not, by itself, provide an adequate meaning to your life, it is one necessary
dimension in a healthy existence. We shouldn't be ashamed of
this. One of the most amazing facts of life is that we have the
opportunity to contribute to our own health and healing. This
power clamors to be put to use.

Still, at least one important issue remains unsettled. Why
does kindness—whether administered to ourselves or others—
heal? The answer: I don't think anyone knows for sure. Or,
more precisely, I don't think anyone has an answer that everyone will accept. No one has yet provided undeniable proof as
to how and why caring leads to improved health and well-
being. We don't know for sure why it works.

Fortunately, we don't need anyone else's approval to prescribe this medicine. Caring never needs clearance from the
Federal Drug Administration. Even though we may not be able
to completely explain its power, we can still use it. And maybe,
if we use it enough, we will come to understand it better.

Perhaps we will each have to come to our own conclusions.
Maybe there are different answers for different people, all of
them true. But I will offer one explanation of how kindness
heals that may be useful to some.

Not long ago, a spokesperson for Alcoholics Anonymous
gave a talk in St. Louis. This gentleman, who appeared to be in

his late sixties, described a life of much suffering. A recovering alcoholic and a member of AA, he used only his first name to preserve his anonymity. He had spent a good deal of his life in prison for a variety of offenses, all committed while intoxicated. Although he came close to death many times, he lived long enough to turn his life around. And in the process he became devoted to helping others turn theirs around too. He indicated that he was trying to take care of himself *and* others. In his own words, he detailed the value of the Great Balancing Act. Specifically, this man said one special thing that may help us here.

This simple statement appeared to help many understand the power of caring. He said, simply, "The closest you will ever come to God while you are on this earth is when you are helping someone." The implications of this are many. And it's probably best if you interpret most of them yourself. One possible interpretation, however, is that the power in caring comes from the involvement of God. To put it differently, caring strengthens your connection with your Higher Power. If this connection becomes strong enough, your power to heal may border on the miraculous.

But who's to say? Why listen to an old drunk who spent most of his years in a dismal relationship with life? Maybe we should merely consider the scientists and the scholars. Perhaps they are the only ones entitled to guide us in matters of consequence. Well, those who feel this way may never understand kindness. Kindness is taught in the most simple and often the most peculiar circumstances. Kahlil Gibran, in fact, once wrote that he learned kindness from the unkind.

There is a special wisdom among people who have survived tragedy, especially those who have survived it well. (You know, those who have lived through severe misfortune and somehow reached the other side a better person.) They know things many of the rest of us don't, because they've been to a place where not all of us have. Lessons learned while there often involve the power of caring. Those who survive well tend to be those who learn how to give and receive compassion. They learn to accept care and treatment for their hurts.

Not everyone, though, survives well. "I do not believe that sheer suffering teaches," wrote Anne Morrow Lindbergh. "To suffering must be added mourning, understanding, patience, love, openness, and the willingness to remain vulnerable. All these and other factors combined, if circumstances are right, can teach and lead to rebirth." Healing requires effort, risk, and the realization that we have the right to care for ourselves and receive care from others.

Through her research with survivors of child abuse, Linda T. Sanford concluded that allowing oneself to receive care and nurturance can be the biggest obstacle for survivors to overcome on the road to recovery. "Although it was often far more difficult, learning to receive love comfortably was as necessary to their healing as having the love they offer accepted as worthy."[13]

Loving your neighbor as yourself doesn't mean much if you are unwilling to love yourself. The Golden Rule is typically spoken to encourage people to care for others, assuming that everyone already loves themselves. But such is not always the case. Erich Fromm was one of many great minds to insist that until we love ourselves, we will be incapable of loving others. Many of these same great minds have also pointed out that too few of us give ourselves permission to love ourselves.

The only one who can give you the green light to love and care for yourself is you. If you do, you will greatly increase your personal power. Not only will you develop your ability to heal, you will also build your power to grow. If you will be kind to yourself, you will be much more likely to find happiness. If you will be kind to others, you will improve the world.

Contented and fulfilled people seem to be those with a deeply rooted conviction that says, "I would like to help us all." (And if that old healing drunk is right, well, then these souls spend a lot of their lives very close to God.)

7

TRANSFORMATIONS

Your vision will become clear only when you can look
into your own heart.

Carl Jung

*P*eople can change. We can make minor alterations in our
lives and we can make the pervasive types of changes that
transform our psyches and our souls. Sometimes we choose to
believe that the big changes are impossible. We do this to
protect ourselves. There's a certain amount of security in rou-
tine. Change means newness. Newness can be frightening.

While we control much of the change that comes in our
lives, there are also some that find us. If you remember, Ebenezer Scrooge didn't invite the three Spirits of Christmas into
his life. But they came anyway, and the changes they helped
make in his life were monumental. It was a transformation, a
journey into a new life.

The Spirits sought out Scrooge and they put the reality he
had ignored right in front of him. This was their job in his
transformation. The change could not have been completed,
however, unless Ebenezer had allowed their message to reach
his core. Scrooge's transformation—like most transformations—could not have run its course until he surrendered himself to a force that gave him a look at what his life could mean.

Scrooge's transformation was a journey to kindness. The
taker became a giver. As special as this process is, the transfor-

121

mation to kindness occurs to people all over the world, every day. Being overwhelmed by and transported to kindness may be the most underreported major life event known to humankind. What happened to the Grinch happens to people all the time. Rarely, however, do we discuss it. It doesn't sound completely sane. Transformations are really a form of healthy insanity. A breakthrough that may seem for a time to be a breakdown, a transformation can radically alter one's relationship with life.

A transformation often begins with an awareness of inner turmoil. A time when we become aware of (perhaps consumed by) the sense that things aren't right.

Questioning our path, though at times difficult, can prepare us for an awakening. At this point, the unexamined life starts being examined and we begin looking for another path, one that provides fulfillment. This is not merely the road that *leads* to fulfillment; it is the avenue that provides direction and purpose *while* we travel it.

A transformation to kindness begins with a reachable moment, a time when (for whatever reason) we are open to being affected by kindness. Sometimes the opening is large and inviting; at other times it starts small and uncertain. In either case, it is an opening and an opportunity to feel the power of kindness.

A transformation is not a passive process. True, something *happens* to the person involved. But that person plays an important role. He must respond to the call and allow himself to be moved. A transformation cannot be completed without the consent of the person involved.

To paraphrase a Zen proverb, when the heart is ready, a teacher appears. When we find ourselves willing to consider a compassionate lifestyle, something comes along to enter that opening. While some of us have lived a completely self-centered, selfish lifestyle and are in need of a major transformation, most folks, I think, are subject to that transformation that takes a good human being and makes him better. Both, of course, are amazing and profound experiences. And both begin with that opening that says we are willing to grow into more caring beings. If we protect this opening, experiences that teach compassion will arrive.

When the heart is ready to grow, our old theories stop making sense. Instead of seeing only the poverty, one starts to notice the generosity. Instead of seeing only the suffering, one begins to recognize the caring. And rather than seeing only the loneliness, one starts to feel the compassion. As a transformation unfolds, the theory that people are out only for themselves just doesn't explain reality anymore. The goodness becomes undeniable. Once the denial is broken, wonderful changes begin to occur.

Rabbi Harold Kushner has written: "When weak people become strong, when selfish people become generous, when timid people become brave—those are miracles."[1] If so, we are in the presence of miracles daily. Sometimes these conversions come on suddenly like a seizure or a bolt of lightning. At other times they are the result of a gradual process that may take place over months or even years. But most often, a transformation is a growing process consisting of a series of small to moderate lightning bolts that sometimes lead to a large grand finale that breaks any remaining denial.

The process usually begins with a heightened awareness of the events in one's life. In A Christmas Carol, the Spirit of Christmas Present tells Scrooge, "I'm beginning to think you've gone through life with your eyes closed. Open them. Open them wide!" The Spirit might well have said, "Begin your transformation!"

As one's awareness increases, one's heart becomes ready. Perhaps more than anything, at this point, one needs courage, the courage to let go of the old, the courage needed to take a leap of faith. This can be a time of fear. Still, facing the fear has its rewards. When we become afraid, we come to a greater appreciation of kindness. We are more easily moved. We remember acts of caring we have received while afraid. Fear frequently serves as the opening that allows us to be touched by kindness.

Fear can produce a reachable moment. It can create an opportunity to be reached and touched by kindness. Also, when we are afraid, we are less likely to be distracted by useless complexity. When we are afraid, we appreciate simplicity. Not the shallow, narrow-minded type, but rather the simplicity that helps us understand simple truths such as: a kind act doesn't need an explanation. When we are afraid and someone helps us, we don't need to demand, "Tell me why you did that." "Thank you" is usually enough.

In order for a transformation to emerge, we need several forces to join in the same place. These are: a growing awareness, a ready heart, fear, courage, teachers, and an appreciation of simplicity. Beyond this, there are forces and qualities unique to each individual. These are the ingredients that address the special needs and circumstances of each human being.

When we realize all the factors that must unite to produce a transformation, we begin to understand Rabbi Kushner's description of this process as a miracle. At the very least it is an amazing coincidence. Choose the term you prefer. I'm not sure there's much of a difference. I've even heard coincidence defined as a miracle in which God wishes to remain anonymous.

Many who have studied personal transformations have emphasized the involvement of the spiritual dimension. Author Emma Bragdon, for instance, instead of focusing on the word *transformation*, prefers to use the phrase *spiritual emergence* to accentuate the spiritual nature of this phenomenon. According to Bragdon,

> Spiritual emergence is a natural process of human development in which an individual goes beyond normal personal feelings and desires—ego—into the *transpersonal*, increasing relatedness, Higher Power, or God. . . . The end result is a positive transformation, observable in increased compassion, creativity, and a desire to be of service to all of life.[2]

An extraordinary example of such an emergence might be Albert Schweitzer. In the early 1900s this young doctor took his training and talents to the place where he felt they were needed most—the jungles of Africa. While there he immersed himself in the care of those who, without him, would probably never have received medical treatment. Working in this environment, he encountered countless hardships. But perhaps most distressing of all was the confusion he experienced while struggling to know if he were following his correct path in life. During this conflict, in an attempt to find his answers, he filled numerous notebooks with his thoughts, hoping that this would eventually give him the clues he sought.

In hindsight we might say that his work and his writing were setting the stage for what was to become a turning point. Already a very good human being devoted to the welfare of humankind, Schweitzer longed for a sign that he was using his life as he should. I guess you could say his heart was ready. Finally his answer came. While crossing a river in a small boat, out in the midst of nature, the words *reverence for life* came to him. Schweitzer knew immediately this was the message he had been waiting and working for.

To understand the meaning of *reverence for life* we need to read the doctor's own words:

> You ask me to give you a motto. Here it is: *service*. Let this word accompany you throughout your life. Let it be before you as you seek your way and your duty in the world. May it be recalled to your minds if ever you are tempted to forget it or set it aside. It will not always be a comfortable companion but it will always be a faithful one. And it will be able to lead you to happiness, no matter what the experiences of your lives are.[3]

It's not only the saintly who have transcendent moments. Recently I had the pleasure of watching a seventeen-year-old young man named Mark go through a powerful transformation.

Before Mark reached his tenth birthday, his parents had gone through a difficult, contested divorce. During the time of the divorce, Mark's parents became caught up so completely in their own emotions that they largely neglected Mark and his younger brother. Without ever being asked, young Mark stepped in and became a surrogate parent to his younger brother. After the divorce, this relationship continued and Mark grew into the caretaker role. Whatever emotional upset he felt about his parents' separation had to be put on hold. He had to be strong.

In the midst of the chaos of his life, Mark found direction and an emotional anchor in his younger brother. They needed each other. In spite of everything, as long as they had each other, life was O.K.

Then came the ultimate tragedy. Mark was eleven at the time and his brother six. Mark ran across the street, and the younger brother followed. Mark wasn't to blame. He couldn't have known. In an instant of screams and screeches his brother was fatally injured. Run over by a drunken driver.

Before his brother lost consciousness for the final time, Mark watched him move his mouth in a desperate attempt to speak his last words. But nothing could be heard. He lapsed into a coma and died later that day. Mark never let go of that memory of the dying child fighting to speak.

Soon after the accident, Mark began using drugs. By the time he was fourteen, he was using them on a daily basis as well as dealing in drugs. He also began to become more violent, mostly schoolyard fights that became an almost everyday occurrence. Before long he began to carry a knife with him. He felt he had created so many enemies for himself that he needed the protection. One might suggest that he was at war with the world. Remarkably, however, Mark experienced few punitive consequences for his behavior. His intelligence helped him get around those kinds of things.

Mark, though, was a runaway train and it was only a matter of time until the day of reckoning came. That day came shortly after his seventeenth birthday. At a party late one night, while intoxicated, Mark got into another fight. Without thinking, he pulled his knife. Within seconds, his opponent lay bleeding on the ground, slashed across the neck and chest.

The ambulance came. The police arrived. The victim left in the ambulance; no one knew if he would survive. Swearing that he didn't care what would become of him, Mark left in handcuffs with the police. Filled with the anger and hostility that grows out of hopelessness, aimlessness, and grief, the hatred inside Mark became uncontrollable. It had turned against him. You could say it controlled him. He wouldn't let anyone get close enough to help him regain his freedom, his hope, his life.

Then the miracles, or coincidences, began. First, in spite of the fact that Mark's victim had originally been given a poor prognosis, he lived. No murder charges. Both boys had a future again. The dead end started to turn into a path once more.

Then came a surprise that to this day cannot be completely explained, and yet, in hindsight, it seems as if fate would not have permitted anything else. Mark pleaded guilty and pre-pared himself to spend time, perhaps a lot of time, in prison. But in a move that surprised even his public defender, Mark received the option of entering substance-abuse treatment in-stead of going to jail.

Maybe the judge was just soft or maybe he saw something in Mark that had long been invisible to others. Whatever the reason, Mark was told that if he cooperated and completed treatment, he would not be incarcerated. Thus he was given a chance to regain his freedom.

As his sentence was explained, Mark's terror turned to relief. As he absorbed the impact of the ruling, his relief started to transform itself into gratitude. I can't say for certain, but I think his transformation began right there. Two events, both out of his control, turned his way. In the process, he faced real fear. While he was incarcerated awaiting trial, his sobriety, combined with the undeniable drama of his situation, led him to an increased awareness of his own nature and circumstances. As a result, he finally began to grieve over his brother's death.

When Mark entered treatment, he was already moving in the right direction. His awareness continued to grow. He worked courageously to turn his life around. As he moved onto firmer ground, he started helping other clients with their treatments. More time passed and he asked to volunteer his time and energies to the Special Olympics. While these changes were taking place, Mark was becoming a spiritual young man. He spoke openly of how he benefited from prayer. Interestingly, he was skillful with his spirituality. He seemed to know intuitively when it was (and when it was not) time to share it with people. He had a talent for identifying reachable moments in others.

Shortly before he completed treatment, Mark asked to speak with me. He told me of all he had learned and the changes in his life. Then he paused and started to choke up. He looked down at the floor. When he again looked up at me, he had a look on his face that I'm not sure I've ever seen before or since. It's only a bit of an exaggeration to suggest that his expression appeared to say: "I'm about to tell you the meaning of life." As crazy as it sounds, I braced myself a little to prepare for what he was about to say.

With a tear and a smile Mark bravely said, "Ya know, Doc, *it's amazing to care.*"

"Yeah, pal, I know," I replied with a grin on my face and a lump in my throat.

Soon after our conversation, I laughed to myself about how I had thought he was going to tell me the purpose of life.

Later I wondered, "Well . . . maybe he did."

One year after Mark and I had this talk, I received a letter from the judge who had sentenced him. Included in the envelope was a copy of a letter the judge had sent to Mark. It congratulated Mark on all he had accomplished. He had not only avoided trouble, he also continued to be a contributor. His life, which was for a time being wasted, had again become amazing.

In her bestselling book *Pathfinders*, Gail Sheehy wrote: "My research offers impressive evidence that we feel better when we attempt to make our world better . . . to have a purpose beyond one's self lends to existence a meaning and direction—the most important characteristic of high well-being." A transformation involves moving *to* the right path and then moving *on* the right path.

This is the path with spirit and heart. This road is not always an easy one. Sometimes it's almost deadly. Like Mark, who teetered on the brink of self-destruction before being transformed, the specter of death can serve as an introduction to the essence of life. While many events can lead to a transformation, and what moves one person may go unnoticed by another, there is at least one phenomenon that makes just about everyone who faces it reconsider their priorities. Death.

The Near-Death Experience

The Near-Death Experience (or NDE) is a controversial matter. Those who believe in it insist that people have died (for short periods of time) and then returned to life after getting a glimpse of the hereafter. Skeptics, however, are equally adamant that any "bright light" or "tunnel" or "overwhelming sensation" is the result of a brain on the brink of death.

From what I gather, there is as yet no way to settle this argument once and for all. Some will continue to see Near-Death Experiences as miraculous and fascinating while others will continue to dismiss them as merely the products of an active imagination or a dying brain. But there is something about these experiences that does lend itself to precise measurement—the aftermath. People who report having the Near-Death Experience frequently tell of profound changes in their lives as a direct result of their experiences.

Psychologist and recognized authority on the Near-Death Experience Kenneth Ring has identified a pattern of change in behavior in the majority of people who have had NDEs. He has found that people "return" with a decreased fear of death, a belief in the existence of a higher force that is unconditionally loving and compassionate, and an increased compassion and strengthened desire to improve the lives of others.[4]

Physician Melvin Morse has also studied NDEs. He is, however, particularly interested in how they apply to children. Like Ring and other researchers in this area, Morse speaks of a beautiful light that contains a powerful message. Consistently, his young subjects who have traveled to the verge of death have come back with stories of the light. Remarkably, the message they receive from the light varies little from patient to patient. The children report how the light advises them on their purpose in life.

"The messages given to these children of the light are not new or controversial," explained Morse. "They are as old as mankind itself and have served as the primary fuel of our great religions:

'Love your neighbor and cherish life.'
'Do unto others as you would have them do unto you.'
'Clean up your own mess.'
'Be the best that you can be.'
'Contribute to society.'
'Be nice, kind, and loving.'"

After examining all the stories he had heard from adults and children who have faced the light, Morse concluded that they are told to "revere life and see the intricate connections throughout the universe."[5] Dr. Schweitzer's message, you will recall, was "reverence for life." And those intricate (vine-like) connections might be the pathways through which the message from the light is passed on.

Being close to death seems to produce, at the very least, a reachable moment. Ironically, in the face of death, we are given the opportunity to be reborn. I believe many people grow dramatically in their final hours. Some say this is how we prepare ourselves for the journey to the afterlife. Maybe, but there's another possible explanation. With death in sight, we become freer to be what we really are. We come into this life prepared to be empathic and compassionate. These inclinations, however, can be destroyed by environments that do not support them. But when death looms, the constraints disappear and we move toward being who and what we were meant to be.

In the face of death, people also have a knack for acquiring humility. Even those who had never seen any use for it come to respect humility's power when they feel their time slipping away. As we noted earlier, humility appears to be an essential dimension of kindness. Facing death is one way of finding humility, the feeling that begins in the soul that says, "I don't need to be better than anyone else. I just want to be helpful . . . and I'm to do what I can."

An encounter with death can lead to a major transformation. Death helps show us what has always been there. The most powerful transformations occur when we touch what has been within us all along—that something inside that was never allowed adequate expression. Once released, it can explode to the surface fueled by energy that has been collected, perhaps, since birth. This experience can be bewildering, and yet it feels quite natural. It feels like the right way to move. It is, ultimately, reassuring and comforting. Like finally finding yourself where you belong.

In a transformation you are transformed into yourself. Perhaps this was best described by a middle-aged man who was a student in one of my classes. This gentleman was going through a transition of his own. In a paper he wrote on kindness, he ended with this:

> I pray someday I might be kind for the same reason the grass is green. I would be kind, for that is what I was made to be.

Why an encounter with death so often produces profound changes in people is largely unknown. There are plenty of theories, but still many questions. What does appear certain, however, is that it *does* have a tremendous impact on those who get close enough to feel it. It realigns one's priorities and can increase one's powers of empathy and courage. Again, when there is empathy and courage, there will be caring.

Finally, I don't think you have to be within earshot of death in order to see and hear your light. The light also seems to speak during what I call Near-Life Experiences (NLEs). These are the moments when we get a look at what life really is. It's the birth of a baby or a majestic sunset. It's the moment when you hear that your loved one will survive the heart attack (or the point when you hear that you will survive yours). It's the instant when you are hit with the awareness: "God, it's a beautiful world!" Even though you may have said this a thousand times before, after an NLE, you feel something new stir within you when you do. The new feeling may be joy, happiness, awe, love, respect, or a reverence for life.

When a wonderful, life-giving event happens while you are in a reachable moment, you will enter into a Near-Life Experience. Those who allow themselves many reachable moments will encounter life most directly. In the course of their lives, they will know many transformations. Each making them better, healthier people. These souls are enriched by both life and death.

Beliefs That Bind

Transformations often begin when your old theories about life no longer make sense. As these beliefs start to shake and crumble, you feel the first signs of an earthquake moving inside you. As the earthquake rumbles throughout your system, it can move parts of you that may have seemed immovable.

The internal earthquake can be an amazingly healthy and healing force. It represents a milestone where we take control of our lives and live them the way we honestly think it is right. The earthquake provides courage and freedom. It carries a message that says each of us is responsible for his or her own choices. If we accept it and move with it, the earthquake leads to personal empowerment.

Although it may seem illogical, we can start the earthquake ourselves. We can seek the strength and personal power produced by this powerful transformation. We do so by looking directly at the beliefs that guide our behaviors and shape our views of the world.

I suppose there are any number of faulty theories that keep people slaves to selfishness. Here I've identified seven specific irrational beliefs that cripple people emotionally and spiritually. I present them as examples. Each of us must examine our own belief systems to see if these or any other damaging notions lie within. We begin to grow or to heal by becoming aware of beliefs that bind us. Awareness moves us toward transformation.

1. *"If I care, I will get hurt."* There is, of course, some truth to this. People who care can be hurt. They expose their feelings and thus can be ridiculed and rejected. There are risks involved with caring.

This becomes a mistaken belief, however, when it pervades one's thinking. When one concludes that pain is the inevitable consequence of caring, one blinds oneself to the realities of life. With the support of a growing amount of research, we can confidently state that kindness improves our physical, mental, and spiritual health. Rationally speaking, the rewards of caring far outweigh the risks.

It's important to note, however, that the belief that caring hurts is often based in reality. People who think this way are frequently the products of childhoods that proved it true. Young children hurt by relationships may carry through life the conviction that getting close to people leads to misery. They can spend their lives obsessed with protecting themselves. Sometimes the fortunate ones have a crack in their armor through which they can be touched, moved, and, finally, healed. Too many others remain safe and suffering.

Caring doesn't have to hurt. And caring itself provides the courage to care. As jungle doctor Tom Dooley once penned, "The reward for service is the strength to serve." Kindness seems to come easier to some than others. Although it's a natural inclination, it can take time to get the hang of it. It starts by working through the fear. Caring doesn't have to hurt.

2. *"Nobody else cares."* The person who says this is usually someone who truly wants to be a good, giving soul but is paralyzed by the fear of being unique. He fears being a white elephant in a herd of a million gray ones. Still, inside, he aches to make his contributions.

With this irrational belief comes a type of tunnel vision with the tunnel focusing on people performing thoughtless and inconsiderate acts. If someone searches for selfishness, she will probably find it. Consequently, the "nobody *else* cares" belief can become a self-fulfilling prophecy. We can blind ourselves to the caring. Then we live in a dreadful self-made world.

Correcting this fallacy means changing the lens through which we view the world. We need a lens that presents the entire picture, the good and the bad. Other people do care. There's a support group called humanity waiting to welcome anyone interested in helping others, even those who are not quite ready to act on their own concerns. People who think no one else cares have a warm place to go when they start to change their minds.

It's never too late to have a change of heart or a change of mind. Who we really are can emerge at any time. Those who have not been true to themselves can become true at any age. Viktor Frankl called this "the defiant power of the human spirit." It's the defiance needed to be a caring soul even during those times when it seems you are surrounded by those who don't care.

3. *"It's all I can do to take care of myself."* This is another belief that typically masks a burning need to contribute. People

who feel this way on the surface tend to avoid conversations about helping those in need. It makes them feel too guilty. They feel guilty because they are avoiding something they know is right.

Individuals who believe this feel a lack of power. They may say, "One person can't make a difference," but what they really mean is: "*I* can't." They don't believe in their own personal power. Until they change their thinking and begin to empower themselves with the conviction that "I can!" they live unhappy, frustrated lives. Furthermore, their unhappiness supports the notion that they have nothing to give.

4. "*If I make my caring known*, something *terrible will happen.*" Sometimes I think that the most common phobia among adults is the fear of that mysterious "something." Although *something* may mean different things to different people, for most it's that vague, shapeless, unknown catastrophe that lies waiting for us. It's even more amorphous than the ghosts we feared as children, yet it has the same superhuman quality that makes it impossible to conquer.

Unfortunately, in spite of its prevalence, there is no cure for the fear of that "something." You cannot defeat "something." There are no exceptions to this rule. *Something always wins.* The lesson here: never fight "something."

There does exist, however, a way to *remove* the fear of "something." But, as I said, it cannot be overcome as long as it is addressed as "something." "Something" cannot be conquered until you learn its real name. You must be specific. When we say we fear "something," we may really be afraid of rejection, intimacy, failure, success, powerlessness, exposure, or even our own emotions. "Something" is unbeatable. But if we move close enough to it to see what it really is, we find that we were never actually dealing with "something" anyway.

In the case of kindness, the "something" that people fear can be incompetence, newness, rejection, or simply being noticed. It can be many things. Some people need the help of a professional counselor to help them identify their "something."

It can also prove beneficial to have someone to help them deal with what they find.

Thinking that something terrible will happen is irrational because "something" doesn't exist. It is a frightening illusion. If you look past this fictitious monster, you will find a fear that can be conquered.

5. *"If I acted kindly, I would be a hypocrite* (because inside I feel selfish)." The person who thinks this way is missing some important information. There is a selfish urge in us all. Generous people are not special forms of life totally free from the desire to put themselves first. They feel it too. They feel the tug to keep their money in their own pockets, their blood in their own veins, and their free time on their own couches. Generous people never completely lose their desire to keep. They feel it just like everyone else.

Generosity is a victory. When it occurs, you feel the triumph, not the hypocrisy. The fact is that selfish beings can become tremendously giving.

We may never fully erase our desire to think of our needs first. Yet anyone who genuinely makes the effort can transcend these limitations. Then we realize that the idea that acting kind makes one a hypocrite is quite absurd. Indeed, acting kind makes one a hero.

6. *"I'm just a selfish person* (and that's all there is to it)." This is a variation on the old myth that people can't change. A miser stays a miser. A miserable person lives out his life as a miserable person. It's sad but, as they say, that's just the way it is. One never becomes free of the box one was placed in.

Those who profess "I'm just a selfish person" are, virtually without exception, unhappy. And this discontent will grow and grow even though it may be repressed or denied for a time. Eventually, however, the pain reaches the surface. You might think that the pain would prompt persons to change their thinking. But this is not always the case. Many times, the bitterness caused by this belief makes a person hold on to it even tighter. It's as if it defeats a person and convinces him that he no longer has the power to change or improve. He then agrees to stay locked in his box.

Thoreau once remarked that "birds never sing in caves." They don't belong there. Likewise, people never find happiness in boxes. Until one releases the mistaken belief that people cannot change, change will not take place. And then this erroneous belief will prove true. We can prove ourselves right by staying miserable.

7. *"I don't know how."* I guess you would have to say that in some, this is only partially irrational. There are people who have been exposed only to small amounts of kindness. An absence of healthy role models can leave people unsure if they are doing it right.

Kindness, however, is largely a natural act. If we remove the barriers, the caring emerges. It's not so much that someone wouldn't know how to be kind; more often the problem is that he or she doesn't have enough confidence to be kind.

Kindness doesn't require special gifts or training. It lives in everyone. You don't teach kindness as much as you touch it. Those who touch the kindness within are those who become kind. Even those who never get the lessons can learn it.

It's important that we do not make kindness too complicated. If you need to know all the whys and hows to kindness, you might be asking for too much. Besides, not all the answers come through thinking. Keep it simple and it will be easier to touch.

In researching this book, I found an abundance of advice on the nature and causes of kindness. From all this information, one simple quote stands out in my mind as one of the most important of all. Philosopher Eric Hoffer once wrote: "Kindness can become its own motive. We are made kind by being kind."

If it is allowed to flower, kindness will grow throughout our lives. We don't really need to learn how; it comes naturally. All we need to do is decide when to begin.

When an erroneous belief is erased, we become freer. This freedom will not necessarily incite a transformation, but it will prepare us for one. Correcting mistaken beliefs provides us with room for growth, room to improve our lives.

Moved by the Spirit

In his play *Our Town*, Thornton Wilder wrote:

> We all know that something is eternal. And it ain't houses, and it ain't names, and it ain't earth, and it ain't even the stars. . . . Everybody knows in their bones that something is eternal, and that something has to do with human beings. All the greatest people that ever lived have been telling us that for five thousand years.

Mr. Wilder was right. At some level, we all know. The stars may not be eternal but there's something inside human beings that is. We can call this something God or, as some prefer, we can call that piece of God that we each carry inside us the spirit. Some folks have their own name for their piece of the eternal. But whatever we call it, we all know it's there.

Some people let the spirit fill them. Others give it only a small room in their basement stuffed way back underneath their arrogance or cowardice. If we give our spiritual dimension the room to grow, we will eventually feel its power. This force can be humbling and, for a time, frightening. But it deserves the opportunity to move into as many areas of our lives as it can. In the final analysis, we are more spiritual than we are physical. Most of what we are can never be grasped, though it can be felt. In the words of Teilhard de Chardin, "We are not human beings having a spiritual experience. We are spiritual beings having a human experience."

In order to come closer to an understanding of kindness, we need to consider some of the ramifications of being spiritual beings. Fortunately, the equation never gets too complex. Genuine caring—the type that doesn't need a payoff—has its roots planted in the spirit. This is why scientists (i.e., psychologists, psychiatrists, anthropologists, sociologists, etc.) have had such a difficult time comprehending altruism. Their standard formulas simply don't apply. In the case of compassion, we are not dealing primarily with the psyche or society; instead we enter the realm of the spirit. Here reinforcements and repressed instinctual drives don't make much sense. People who are moved by the spirit are kind because this is what the spirit asks. And when they respond to the spirit they feel the most powerful reward known to humankind—the feeling that comes when the spirit and the human are in harmony.

Albert Schweitzer recommended: "Impart as much as you can of your spiritual being to those who are on the road with you, and accept as something precious what comes back to you from them." Your spiritual being grows as it is shared. That "something precious," Schweitzer well knew, is the spirit.

We can develop our spiritual dimension by sharing it. Consequently, transformations can be well within our control. We can create them. As the spirit knows no bounds, it can grow (in small or large steps) forever. Share your love of life and you will love life even more. Share your gratitude and you will become more grateful. Share your courage and you will always possess the courage you need. And hold on to Hoffer's remark: "We are made kind by being kind."

We can control many of our transformations. But not all. Some transformations come uninvited. Unexpected transformations push people to get moving. These sometimes reluctant travelers are compelled to deal with aspects of life that they previously avoided. Feelings that never received attention now demand recognition. Realities that were ignored now become too large to deny. In the process, old feelings and realities are crushed by the earthquake and new ones gradually emerge. If we move with the quake, we find ourselves in a better place. If we refuse to accept the transformation, however, we become shaken, unstable, and fearful.

When people refuse to accept a transformation, they enter into conflict with their spiritual being. This conflict leads nowhere. The spirit can have tremendous power. While I don't know if anyone completely understands why the spirit begins to move within, it seems clear that when it does stir, it acts with a force so strong that even the most desperate efforts to deny it prove ineffective. The force produces a calling that says now is the time to begin being a better human being.

Transformations become crises when they are resisted. When accepted as vital messages they can elevate us to a higher, healthier level of existence. The key is acceptance.

It's easier to accept changes, however significant, when they result from deliberate, premeditated decisions. We feel more in control and thus less threatened. But when the spirit starts to move without our say-so and we feel pushed or pulled in a direction that may be completely new to us, life can become bewildering. Before we begin the struggle to fight our way back to the way we were, we need to consider if this movement might be carrying us to the right path.

In short, the spirit has a force of its own, a powerful force. We don't know all the reasons it moves when it does. It's not clear how the spirit selects its time to move. It does, however, appear to choose wisely.

There's certainly a lot we don't know about when the spirit decides to move. But this is not to say we are completely in the dark. Some things are clear.

One important clue involves the relationship between humility and the spirit. Humbling experiences, we know, serve as invitations for the spirit to enter our awareness. We may find ourselves moved by the spirit at precisely those times when our bodies are broken or our psyches are overwhelmed. It's the loss of a job, a serious illness, or the loss of a loved one that can move us to a place that welcomes the spirit. We cannot know real power until we have known powerlessness. This is what humility is about. Accepting human limitations. Paradoxically, with this acceptance comes personal power.

The spirit offers to pick us up after we encounter experiences so powerful that we are forced to give up our spot in the center of the universe. These are the moments when many of us begin to really consider that part of life that is eternal. In some folks, in fact, it seems that the spirit delays its move until the body and the mind are too weak or too distracted to fight it anymore.

Transformations come in all shapes and sizes. We can decide to enter them or they can choose to enter us. We can cooperate or resist. But keep this in mind. We all have a piece of the eternal inside us. This is the part of humanity that runs through each of us and unites us with one another. Feeling the spirit means feeling the connection. Once aware of this connection, we are moved to kindness. As we become increasingly aware of the Vine that joins us, our caring grows. As Gerald G. Jampolsky insightfully noted, "I can be of no real help to another unless I see that the two of us are in this together, that all of our differences are superficial and meaningless, and that only the countless ways we are alike have any importance at all."[6]

Resisting the spirit produces confusion and bitterness. Accepting it leads to empowerment, serenity, and a more perfect kindness.

8

GRATITUDE

Gratitude—the memory of the heart.
Anonymous

She sat there motionless, wrapped in a blanket that covered her from head to toe. She was the picture of hopelessness. At fifteen years of age, Sandy had just been admitted, for the sixth time, to an inpatient treatment center to help her deal with what she called "my problem."

Some of her hospitalizations were for psychiatric reasons; the others were aimed at treating her drug and alcohol abuse. When I spoke with her, she had little hope that this stay would be any more successful than her previous five.

In spite of a very low self-esteem, Sandy was intelligent, insightful, attractive, and in good physical health. Ironically, one of her difficulties was that she could provoke jealousy among her agemates. She also angered people because of her stealing. She had a tendency to take what she wanted.

After I had gotten to know her a bit, she asked me, "What do you think's wrong with me?"

I took a second to find a better answer but realized I had only one honest reply. "I don't know, Sandy. I really don't know."

142

She responded with a slight nod as if she appreciated the candor and then asked, "What did all those other doctors say was the matter with me?"

So I explained to her that she had been consistently diagnosed as suffering from what is called "major depression," and I tried my best to interpret to her what this meant. But what became immediately apparent was her indifference to my explanation.

"I've heard that all before, ya know," she said with a shrug.

"Yeah, I'm not surprised," I replied.

Then, after a brief period of silence, she added in a thoughtful way, "I don't think that's what's wrong with me."

"What *do* you think is wrong with you, Sandy?" I wondered aloud.

She paused again and then started to cry. "Ya see, *I've never been grateful for my life.*"

She offered no more than that. My first reaction was to think, "If *only* that were all there were to this!" But before long, her insight began to move me. For a long time I have been interested in the relationship between values and mental health. Until Sandy, however, I never really considered how human beings function without gratitude.

A week or so after my conversation with Sandy, I encountered another lesson on gratitude. As I drove into a crowded intersection in St. Louis, I saw a man standing on the median beneath the stoplight. He held a sign that wasn't legible until I pulled alongside him. It read:

HOMELESS
WILL WORK FOR FOOD
THANK YOU

This middle-aged man stood there silently, patiently. His work clothes were old and yet they appeared as if he had taken good care of them. There was something sincere, even powerful about his presence. He wasn't looking for a handout; he

144 · The Joy of Kindness

was looking for work. He wasn't badgering or intimidating; he was hoping for an opportunity.

Perhaps most importantly, this noble poor man added the words "Thank You" to his message. He had no apparent worldly possessions, yet somehow his gratitude survived. There he stood, for the world to see, worn yet grateful.

After watching this fellow, I had a flashback to that ragged man in the old jalopy who stopped on that freezing Indiana highway and repaired my car.

I wasn't sure why one would remind me of the other. One man was black and the other white. There was little about their appearance that might connect them in my mind. Still, something made them neighbors in my memory. Two human beings whose values survived what looked like hard times. The man with seemingly nothing to give personified generosity. The man with seemingly nothing at all personified gratitude.

Then the light came on. The connection between the two experiences is this: gratitude and generosity are themselves related. To understand generosity, we must understand gratitude. More importantly, if we feel gratitude and if we have enough courage, we will act generously. Generosity has its roots in gratitude.

The most common myth about gratitude is that some people are more entitled to it than others. In truth, it lives in anyone who values it and continues to thrive as long as it is welcome. It can be found glowing in rich and poor, kings and common folks. The potential for gratitude lives in everyone, always. Although we can show children how to say thank you, gratitude (like kindness itself) really isn't something you teach, it's something you touch. There are moments when we begin to understand that there is something beyond us responsible for what we've been given. It's also at these times that we start to see *what* we've been given.

Sandy understood this. Somehow she knew that until she could feel gratitude, she would not know real happiness. She may also have identified the first stage in developing gratitude—*becoming grateful for your life.* This is the one thing we all have to be grateful for. Once we feel this gratitude, we start to gain awareness of our other blessings. A by-product of this is an increased self-confidence and self-respect. It's by the light from the flame of gratitude that we see what we have been given. Sandy, it seems, lived in the dark.

Besides being a force in building character, gratitude is the first ingredient in generosity. Gratitude incites generosity. It moves within us the desire to give. For example, I recently received a publication from my alma mater, Boston College, concerning their fund-raising campaign. A portion of the report included interviews with a number of the school's benefactors in an effort to understand why people who give, give.

It didn't take a college education to see the common thread. Their generosity stemmed from their gratitude for what the school had done for them. This, I believe, is the same reason all colleges receive alumni support. This also explains all types of giving. People contribute when they feel grateful. If we feel grateful for our lives, we contribute to life. Maybe Bill W., the cofounder of Alcoholics Anonymous, said it best: "When brimming with gratitude, one's heartbeat must surely result in outgoing love, the finest emotion that we can ever know."

Those who feel gratitude certainly receive psychological rewards. They feel a healthy appreciation for what they've been given, and the generosity that ensues instills a sense of competence and usefulness. Furthermore, it produces a powerful awareness of being connected with humanity. In short, gratitude helps provide security, direction, and self-worth. And, as Bill W. pointed out, gratitude may indeed be the essence of love.

But there is even more to it. Gratitude also feeds the spirit. Ralph Waldo Emerson once wrote: "God enters by a private door into every individual." While I believe this is quite true, I have noticed that human beings have some important spiritual traits in common. We each have the opportunity to bring God into our lives through our own private doors. But as a people, there seem to be at least two occasions where we all tend to open our spiritual doors. We move toward inviting God into our lives, perhaps more than at any other times, when we are filled with feelings of fear and when we are touching feelings of gratitude. So often when we address God, there is a "Help me" or a "Thank you" on the front of it. Although there are many paths to God, need and gratitude seem to be two of the most traveled. If we were a more grateful people, I think we would be a more spiritual people.

Gratitude deepens the spirit. Meister Eckhart believed that the most important prayer in the world was composed of two words: "Thank you." When we touch gratitude, we touch the spirit. People in need of spiritual healing are sometimes advised to write gratitude lists. Building this list means taking the time to examine one's life to find the people, events, and experiences that cause one to feel grateful. Creating this list may require one to spend time in solitude, away from noise and distraction.

You can start your gratitude list, but it would be incorrect to say that you will ever finish it. Once you begin to feel gratitude, *really* feel it, it begins to grow. Your list is long enough when you reach the state where your gratitude is always there, never too far away to be touched. But be warned, this phenomenon can lead to major changes in your life. You may experience a Gratitude Rush. This can sometimes be overwhelming. Though it may feel like an emotional breakdown, it is in fact a tremendous breakthrough, a life-giving transformation.

A Gratitude Rush comes to you when (deep down in your bones) you feel thankful for your life. People in love feel this way. So do parents when they watch their children sleeping at night. People who have experienced the Rush love it. It's a Near-Life Experience that brings one closer to the essence of life. Those who, as adults, are hit with it for the first time may fear it, because they think they are going crazy. It's that strong!

Gratitude may overwhelm you but it will never kill you. It may move you in ways you've never known, but it will never make you lonely or insane. It can be frightening in the same way that a healing force can be frightening to someone who has never healed. It's new and powerful and it produces change.

Gratitude, like empathy, gives us a mighty push toward generosity. Generosity is how we act on our gratitude. Gratitude is not something that can be put completely into words, nor will it ever be, nor would we want it to be. If it could be talked out, it might not need to be acted out. But since it cannot be talked out, it must be acted out.

Generous people usually have some difficulty explaining their motives. This is as it should be. Folks powered by gratitude have a mission, not an explanation. When they explain their kindnesses with brief statements like "I just want to give something back," please understand that this is all that need be said.

If you don't understand this, think about writing your own gratitude list. Then maybe you will understand.

The Fear of Generosity (FOG)

Once unleashed, generosity can take off like a rocket. It feels so right that it can become more addictive than gambling or drugs. Because, at some level, we all know the power of generosity, many of us are afraid to nurture it. Selfishness, at least in the short run, offers more control. Stinginess comes with a lock box for every penny and emotion. They are all in their place and can each be accounted for. But generosity changes this. The locks are destroyed and the lids fly off. Everything that was imprisoned now moves in freedom.

Generosity means building something. We are natural-born builders. We take right to it. As we age, however, this enjoyable behavior often gives way to the adult fear that we may come to like it too much. The urge to build is so strong that some fear it will get out of hand. The fear can become so great that it clouds one's thinking. When clear thought ceases, the real trouble begins. A confused, fear-soaked mind tends to reach rigid and mistaken conclusions. In this case, it may conclude that generosity leads to problems and that the only way to prevent this is to repress the urge to build. We can call this condition Fear of Generosity or just plain FOG.

People lost in the FOG are aimless and discontented. Like those who avoid life in order to avoid the fear of life, people in the FOG try to shut themselves down. They must deny every part of their world that says, in one way or another, "We need your help." Denying such a large portion of reality makes one more than a little crazy. If, by accident, part of the needy world does catch their eye, they must refuse to empathize. If they should see and feel the need, their only way out is through cowardice. (Something they would rather not acknowledge.)

To avoid generosity, we must deny large portions of reality, attempt to strangle empathy, and be prepared to deal with cowardice. Beyond this, we would need to live without gratitude. Even if we could accomplish the first three, gratitude would still threaten to return generosity to our lives. So no gratitude lists allowed here.

To be fair to all those who live in the fear of generosity, I will repeat that generosity should come with a warning. Generosity is a force that can take off on you. It can turn into a life mania or euphoria that can bring about sudden, drastic changes. These changes can scare many of us.

Then there's the issue of compassion fatigue. Good human beings can burn themselves out. Without caution, we can forget the power of generosity and wind up with nothing more to give. Cynicism can accompany this burnout. In some cases, warm, caring, well-intentioned givers end up cold and selfish cynics. Generosity requires that we listen to our heads as well as our hearts.

Philosopher Blaise Pascal contended that the heart has its reasons which reason knows nothing of. We could say that listening to the heart leads to a healthy insanity. Even when it is tempered by reason, the heart warms our lives and adds a spontaneity that may appear a little crazy to an overly civilized individual (i.e., someone who listens *only* to reason). Giving away some of your money can seem like sheer lunacy to a miser. But this behavior is, in fact, anything but demented. On the contrary, eminent psychiatrist Karl A. Menninger stated clearly that "generous people are rarely mentally ill people." Alfred Adler and many other authorities on the health of the human mind and spirit have also insisted that health and happiness are the product of more than pure reason. The feelings of belonging and connectedness that are the foundation of mental, emotional, and spiritual health can be achieved only by those brave souls who free themselves from the tyranny of reason. It takes real courage to loosen one's grip on reason and allow for spontaneous feelings of wonder, empathy, humor, love, gratitude, and generosity.

People who walk through the fear of generosity deserve what they find. They find a mission and a sense of belonging in a world they are building. As they build, they grow stronger and more alive. They feel more connected with life. Paradoxically, as they grow mightier, they gather more humility. They gain a clearer view of what needs to be done.

The fear of generosity is based on the mistaken belief that generosity is a form of self-destruction when, in truth, generosity is most certainly an act of creation. It empowers the body, mind, and spirit. Look at the world around you. Decide how you will leave your mark. Choose what you will build. And never let your fear make your decisions for you.

Building a Better World

Kindness may be the most simple way to improve the world. Every kind deed impacts the planet. It influences the present, the future. There are no insignificant acts of caring. Act as if what you do makes a difference; it surely does, remarked William James.

Understanding kindness means accepting our personal power. If you see your place in the universe, *really see it*, you will *not* be struck by your insignificance. Rather, *you will be awed by your significance and your power to build and contribute.* The effects of your generosity will be felt beyond your place and time. Each act of compassion is handed to the world as well as to the next generation to build upon. With each kindness, the spirit becomes deeper and the branches of the Vine grow stronger.

If I have learned one thing in writing this book, it is that caring people have a special wisdom. Included in this wisdom is the knowledge that humankind is in need of their contributions. They see, hear, and feel the need. They are not intimidated or paralyzed by the awareness that they cannot offer all that is needed. They can do only what they can do.

This lesson is conveyed beautifully in Anatole France's story of the young monk who desperately wanted to express his gratitude and devotion to the Virgin Mary. At the monastery, he watched the others play wonderful music, recite marvelous poetry, and sing in magnificent voices to honor her. He knew he could do none of these. The only special skill this novice had learned prior to entering the monastery was to entertain modestly as a juggler. And so, in the dead of the night, driven by the need to serve, walking quietly so as not to be seen and mocked by his brothers, he made his way to the altar with his bag of balls and wooden mallets, and did his act for Our Lady.[1] Fueled by gratitude, he did what he could do.

The image of a simple juggler applying his craft in front of the altar in a dark church seems so honest and moving. This young monk, who gave all he had, is the type of hero with whom we can all identify. He had no riches or superhuman powers, just a small talent with the willingness to serve. He didn't wait to win the lottery before giving what he could.

Deep inside himself, I think, he knew there was no excuse for waiting to express his gratitude.

Shortly before his death, in his book *Oh, the Places You'll Go!*, Dr. Seuss described an awful spot called the Waiting Place. This, he knew, is "a most useless place." People who live here just wait for things. Things like trains, planes, snow, a yes, a no, or for their hair to grow. They wait for their Uncle Jake, a Better Break, a pair of pants, or Another Chance. In the Waiting Place, "everyone is just waiting."

In the Waiting Place, you might say, people wait for the opportunity to be significant, to make a worthwhile contribution. But, of course, there is no reason to wait. It's always our turn to move. We are all in the front of the line.

Remember that back in chapter 1 we discussed the research that indicates how people tend to follow examples of kindness. If the person at the front of the line at the check-out in the supermarket drops some money in the canister for charities, the odds greatly increase that the others in line will do so as well. Well, maybe it's best if we live our lives like we are first in the kindness line. That our actions may have an impact on the behavior of others. Because they undoubtedly will.

Sometimes it seems that God's greatest gift to humankind is that He made kindness so simple. Anyone can learn it. Anyone can share it. Still, kindness makes people extraordinary. It offers us the way and the power to find the joy and meaning of life.

NOTES

Preface
1. H. J. Brown, *Live and Learn and Pass It On* (Nashville, Tenn.: Rutledge Hill Press, 1992), p. 106.

Chapter 1
1. M. Hunt, *The Compassionate Beast* (New York: William Morrow & Co., 1980), p. 21.
2. Ibid., p. 96.
3. In A. Kohn, *The Brighter Side of Human Nature* (New York: Basic Books, 1990), p. 243.
4. Hunt, *The Compassionate Beast*, p. 13.
5. Kohn, *The Brighter Side of Human Nature*, p. 64.
6. R. Ardrey, *The Social Contract* (New York: Dell Publishing Co., 1971).
7. F. Flach, *Resilience* (New York: Fawcett Columbine, 1988), p. 216.

Chapter 2
1. B. Bettelheim, *The Uses of Enchantment* (New York: Vintage Books, 1976), p. 125.
2. H. A. Hornstein, *Cruelty and Kindness* (Englewood Cliffs, N.J.: Prentice-Hall, 1976), p. 47.
3. M. R. Yarrow, P. M. Scott, and C. Z. Waxler, "Learning Concern for Others," *Developmental Psychology* 47:118–25.
4. N. Eisenberg and P. H. Mussen, *The Roots of Prosocial Behavior in Children* (New York: Cambridge University Press, 1989), p. 69.
5. S. P. Oliner and P. M. Oliner, *The Altruistic Personality* (New York: The Free Press, 1988), p. 249.
6. Ibid., pp. 249–50.
7. Eisenberg and Mussen, *The Roots of Prosocial Behavior in Children*, p. 65.

8. E. Staub, *Positive Social Behavior and Morality* (New York: Academic Press, 1979).

Chapter 3
1. In T. Adler, "Even Babies Empathize, Scientists Find; But Why?" *American Psychological Association Monitor*, June 1990, p. 9.
2. In Kohn, *The Brighter Side of Human Nature*, p. 49.
3. C. D. Batson, "How Social an Animal?" *American Psychologist* 45:344.
4. Flach, *Resilience*, p. 35.
5. Ibid., p. 35.
6. Batson, *"How Social an Animal?"* p. 344.
7. I. Flores, "Auschwitz Survivor Helps Terminally Ill Children," Kissimee, Fla.: *Associated Press*, August 10, 1990.

Chapter 4
1. "For Victims, Flood Means Sharing," *St. Louis Post-Dispatch*, May 9, 1990.
2. "Rooting for Grocer," *St. Louis Post-Dispatch*, May 7, 1990.
3. In Hunt, *The Compassionate Beast*, p. 26.
4. Oliner and Oliner, *The Altruistic Personality*, p. 177.
5. Ibid., p. 178.
6. G. G. Jampolsky, *Teach Only Love* (New York: Bantam Books, 1983), p. 2.
7. E. Fromm, *The Anatomy of Human Destructiveness* (New York: Fawcett Publications, 1973), p. 355.
8. Hornstein, *Cruelty and Kindness*, p. 117.
9. A. M. Pines, "What Makes a Couple Happy?" *Redbook*, April 1990, p. 103.
10. H. Kushner, *Giving Meaning to Life* (Washington, D.C.: Washington Institute of Contemporary Issues, 1988), p. 60.

Chapter 5
1. L. B. Smedes, *Forgive and Forget* (New York: Pocket Books, 1984), p. 110.
2. Ibid., p. 45.
3. Jampolsky, *Teach Only Love*, p. 110.
4. C. Black, *It's Never Too Late to Have a Happy Childhood* (New York: Random House, 1989).

Chapter 6
1. B. S. Siegel, *Peace, Love and Healing* (New York: Harper & Row, 1989), p. 119.

2. J. J. Lynch, *The Broken Heart: The Medical Consequences of Loneliness* (New York: Basic Books, 1977), p. 181.
3. J. S. House, C. Robbins, and H. L. Metzner, "The Association of Social Relationships and Activities with Mortality: Predictive Evidence from the Tecumseh Community Health Study," *American Journal of Epidemiology* 116:123–40.
4. M. Seligman, *Learned Optimism* (New York: Alfred A. Knopf, 1991), p. 288.
5. D. Dinkmeyer and L. E. Losoncy, *The Encouragement Book: Becoming a Positive Person* (Englewood Cliffs, N.J.: Prentice-Hall, 1980), p. 7.
6. J. Segal, *Winning Life's Toughest Battles* (New York: Ivy Books, 1986), p. 113.
7. J. Segal, *Coping with Life's Crises* (Washington, D.C.: Washington Institute of Contemporary Issues, 1987), p. 60.
8. M. James and J. James, *Passion for Life* (New York: E. P. Dutton, 1991), p. 187.
9. Dr. Seuss, *Oh, the Places You'll Go!* (New York: Random House, 1990).
10. B. S. Siegel, *Love, Medicine, and Miracles* (New York: Harper & Row, 1986), p. 94.
11. Kohn, *The Brighter Side of Human Nature*, p. 121.
12. L. T. Sanford, *Strong at the Broken Places* (New York: Random House, 1990), p. 135.
13. Ibid., p. 142.

Chapter 7
1. H. Kushner, *Giving Meaning to Life* (Washington, D.C.: Washington Institute of Contemporary Issues, 1988), p. 31.
2. E. Bragdon, *The Call of Spritual Emergency* (San Francisco: Harper & Row, 1990), p. 1.
3. In P. Ferucci, *Inevitable Grace* (Los Angeles: Jeremy P. Tarcher, 1990), p. 81.
4. In Bragdon, *The Call of Spiritual Emergency*, p. 14.
5. M. Morse and P. Perry, *Closer to the Light* (New York: Villard Books, 1990), p. 163.
6. G. G. Jampolsky, *Love Is Letting Go of Fear* (Berkeley, Calif.: Celestial Arts, 1979), p. 6.

Chapter 8
1. In W. F. Buckley, *Gratitude: Reflections on What We Owe Our Country* (New York: Random House, 1990), p. xiii.